Program Design 2.0

--The Structure-Behavior Coalescence Approach--

William S. Chao

Structure-Behavior Coalescence

Software Architecture = Software Structure + Software Behavior

CONTENTS

PREFACE

Program design (or software program design) is, in the software systems development, the design and implementation phase. That is, program design means to get a solution to furnish customers' requirements on the software system. When working on the program design, we mainly consider how to manufacture the software system, but not to specify what this software system is.

A software system has been designed hopefully to be an integrated whole, embodied in its assembled components, their interactions with each other and the environment. Since software structure and software behavior are the two most prominent views of a software system integrating the software structure and software behavior apparently is the best way to achieve a truly integrated whole of a software system. Because program design 1.0 does not design the integration of software structure and software behavior, very likely it will never be able to actually form an integrated whole of a software system.

Structure-behavior coalescence (SBC) provides an elegant way to integrate the software structure and software behavior, and hence achieves a truly integrated whole, of a software system. A truly integrated whole sets a path to achieve the desired program design. SBC facilitates an integrated whole. Therefore, we conclude that program design 2.0 using the SBC approach, which contains three fundamental diagrams: a) framework diagram, b) component operation diagram and c) interaction flow diagram, is highly adequate in designing a software system.

ABOUT THE AUTHOR

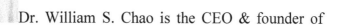

Dr. William S. Chao is the CEO & founder of SBC Architecture International®. SBC (Structure-Behavior Coalescence) architecture is a systems architecture which demands the integration of systems structure and systems behavior of a system. SBC architecture applies to hardware architecture, software architecture, enterprise architecture, knowledge architecture and thinking architecture. The core theme of SBC architecture is: "Architecture = Structure + Behavior."

William S. Chao received his bachelor degree (1976) in telecommunication engineering and master degree (1981) in information engineering, both from the National Chiao-Tung University, Taiwan. From 1976 till 1983, he worked as an engineer at Chung-Hwa Telecommunication Company, Taiwan.

William S. Chao received his master degree (1985) in information science and Ph.D. degree (1988) in information science, both from the University of Alabama at Birmingham, USA. From 1988 till 1991, he worked as a computer scientist at GE Research and Development Center, Schenectady, New York, USA.

PART I: BASIC CONCEPTS

Chapter 1: Introduction to Program Design

A software systems development carries out the work flow steps and therefore may also be called software process. We need to define a software process in order to engineer a software system correctly from start to finish. The software process can be divided into five phases: a) project planning, b) requirements and specifications, c) design and implementation, d) verification and validation and e) product evolution.

Program design (or software program design) is, in the software process, the design and implementation phase. That is, program design means to get a solution to furnish customers' requirements on the software system. When working on the program design, we mainly consider how to manufacture the software system, but not to specify what this software system is.

1-1 Software Development Process

A software systems development carries out the work flow steps and therefore may also be called software development process [Pres09, Somm06, Your99]. We need to define a software development process in order to engineer a software system correctly from start to finish. The software development process, as shown in Figure 1-1, can be divided into five phases: a) project planning, b) requirements and specifications, c) design and implementation, d) verification and validation and e) product evolution.

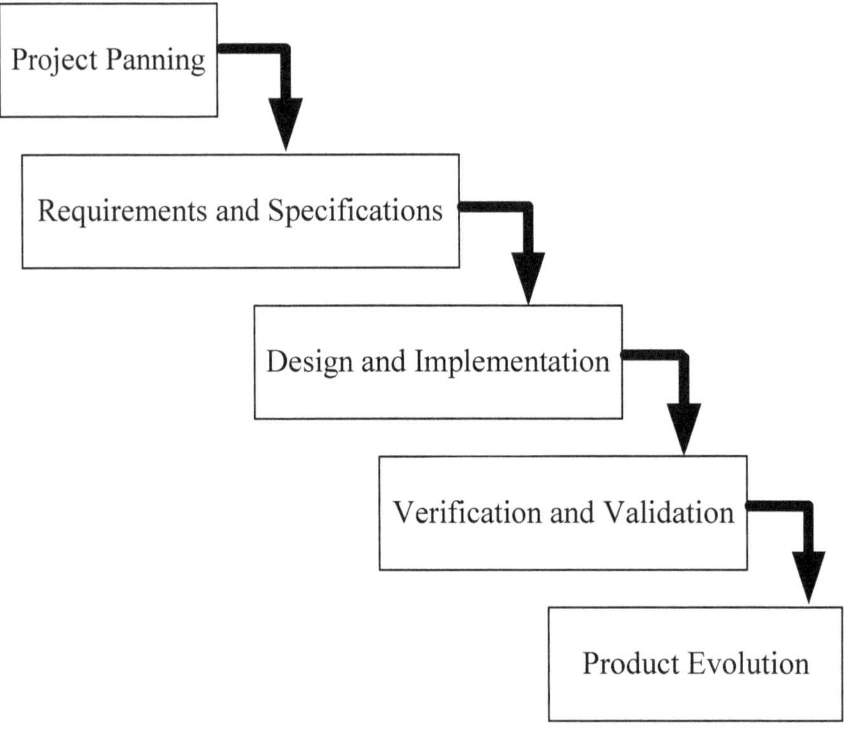

Figure 1-1　Five Phases of the Software Development Process

1-1-1 Project Planning

Project planning determines the general goals of the software development project. These general goals include: project scope determination; selection of the software process model; selection of the software engineering development technology; estimating applicable resources; determining software metric methodology; cost estimation; risk management; project scheduling and tracking; determining the configuration management approach; understanding the level of quality management; choosing software engineering tools; drawing up contracts; and determining post-project follow up.

1-1-2 Requirements and Specifications

The requirements and specifications phase consists of determining what the customer really requires. Requirements and specifications appertain to the problem space. When working on requirements and specifications, we usually only specify what the software system is, but never think about how this software system shall be manufactured.

1-1-3 Design and Implementation

The design and implementation phase belongs to the solution space. In other words, design and implementation try to secure a solution to meet or exceed customer requirements. It is opposite to requirements and specifications, design and implementation mainly consider how to manufacture this software system, but not to specify what this software system is.

1-1-4 Verification and Validation

The fourth step is called the verification and validation, abbreviated as V&V, phase. Verification uses proving technology. Validation uses testing technology. After the software product has been manufactured, we use either verification or validation to determine if or not the software product meets the requirements and specifications initially settled.

1-1-5 Product Evolution

Product evolution is the fifth, also the last, phase of software process. After verification and validation, we hand over the software product for the customer to use. Uses for several years, several month or even several days later, if has the necessity to carry on the next edition, either perceive that some part of wrong, some parts need the reinforcement, either the customer thinks that some places must change the requirements and specifications, even overhauls greatly, then must carry on the product evolution in accordance.

1-2 Program Design

Program design (or software program design) [Jack75] may refer to all the activities involved in conceptualizing, framing, implementing, commissioning and ultimately modifying complex software systems.

Program design is, in the software development process, the design and implementation phase. That is, design and implementation endeavor to get a solution to furnish customers' requirements. When working on the program design, we mainly consider how to manufacture this software system, but not to specify what this software system is.

During the design and implementation phase, both analysts and designers need to coordinate closely, exchange the opinion fully, finally achieve the program design document output, as shown in Figure 1-2.

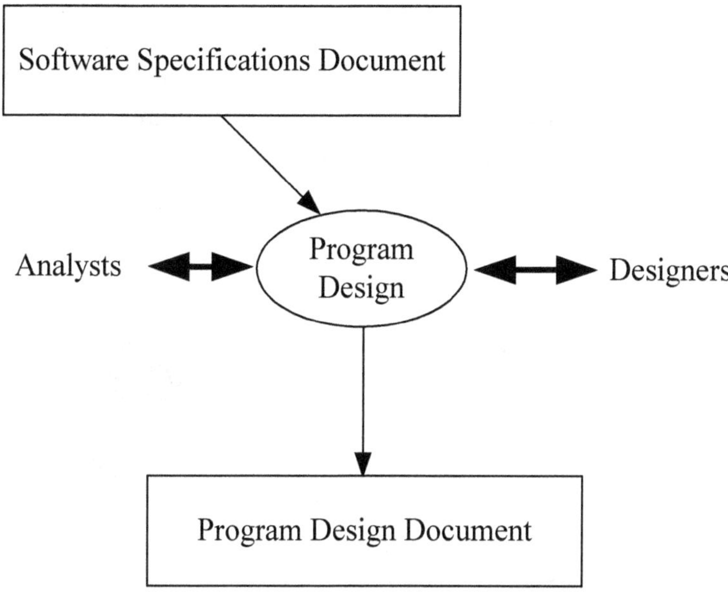

Figure 1-2 Work of Design and Implementation

Analysts maintain notable responsibility in the program design work. The analyst besides provides the specifications document to the designer, but also needs to exchange the opinion with the designer, to check the rationality of the customer's request.

Designers also uphold grand responsibility in the program design work. The designer must possess the capability of deriving a sturdy software system from the specifications document. In addition, the designer also is accountable to bring together the program design document.

1-3 Multiple Views of a Software System

In general, a software system is extremely complex that it consists of multiple views such as structure view, behavior view, function view, data view as shown in Figure 1-3 [Denn08, Kend10, Pres09, Somm06].

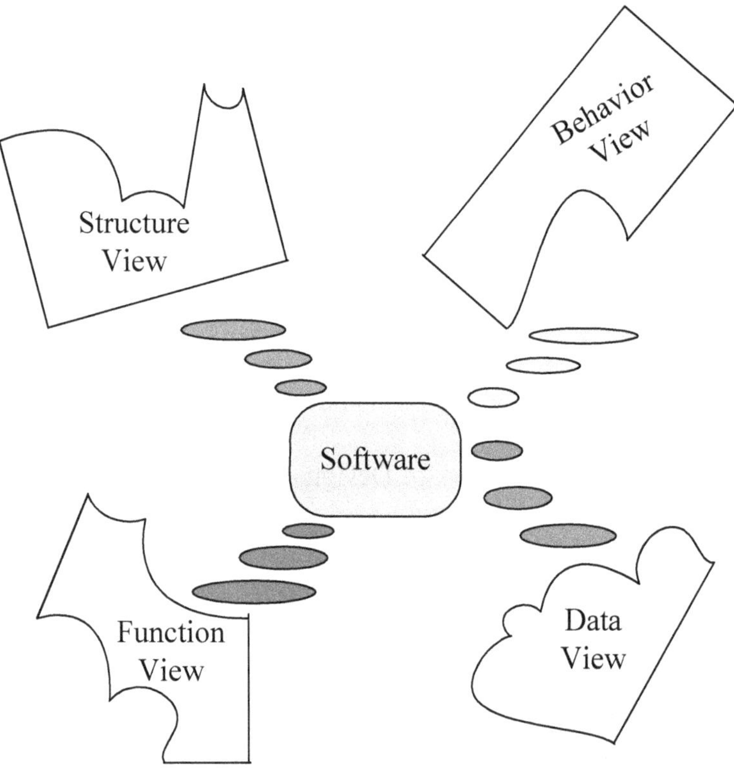

Figure 1-3 Multiple Views of a Software System

Among the above multiple views, the structure and behavior views are perceived as the two prominent ones. The structure view focuses on the software structure which is described by components and their composition while the behavior view concentrates on the software behavior which involves interactions [Chao15a, Chao15b, Chao15c, Chao15d, Chao15e, Hoar85, Miln89, Miln99] among the external environment's actors and components. Function and data views are considered to be other views as shown in Figure 1-4.

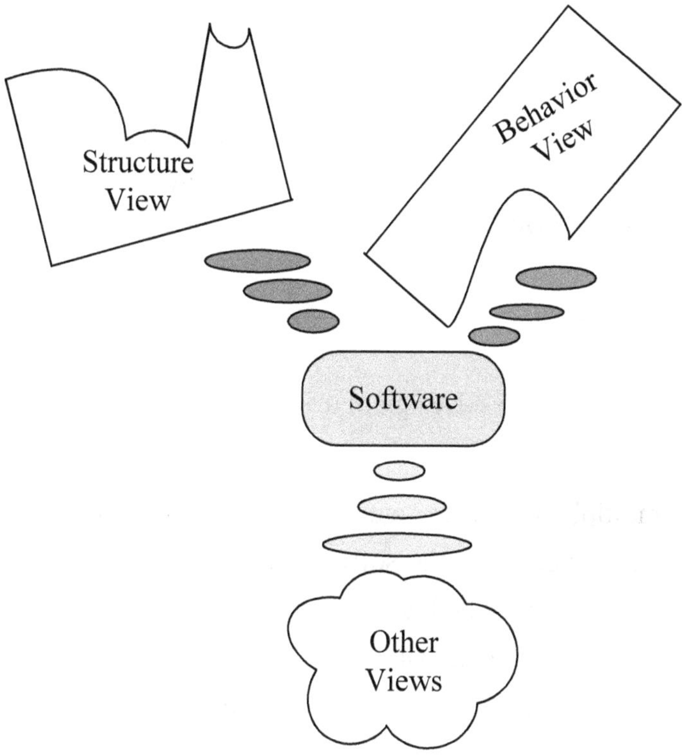

Figure 1-4 Structure, Behavior and Other Views

Either Figure 1-3 or Figure 1-4 represents the multiple views of a software system. In some situations Figure 1-3 is used and in other situations Figure 1-4 is used.

Accordingly, a software system is designed in Figure 1-5 to be an integrated whole of that software's multiple views, i.e., structure, behavior and other views, embodied in its assembled components, their interactions [Chao15a, Chao15b, Chao15c, Chao15d, Chao15e, Hoar85, Miln89, Miln99] with each other and the environment. Components are sometimes labeled as non-aggregated systems, parts, entities, objects and building blocks [Chao14a, Chao14b, Chao14c].

A software system is an integrated whole of that software's multiple views, i.e., structure, behavior, and other views, embodied in its assembled components, their interactions with each other and the environment.

Figure 1-5 Design of a Software System

Since multiple views are embodied in the software's assembled components which belong to the software structure, they shall not exist alone. Multiple views must be loaded on the software structure just like a cargo is loaded on a ship as shown in Figure 1-6. There will be no multiple views if there is no software structure. Stand-alone multiple views are not meaningful.

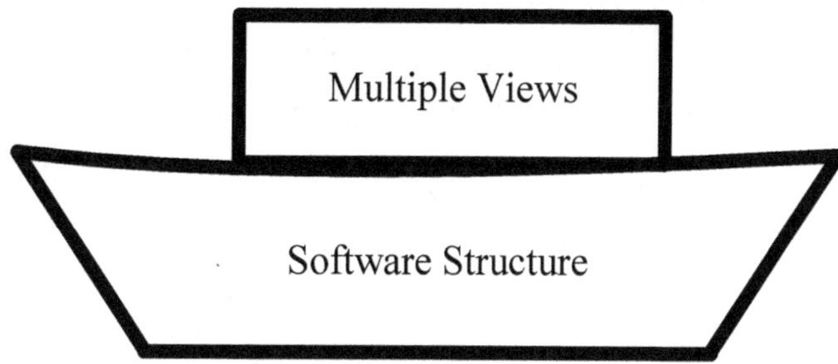

Figure 1-6 Multiple Views Loaded on the Software Structure

1-4 Multiple Views Non-Integrated Approaches for Program Design 1.0

When designing a software system, the multiple views non-integrated approach, also known as the model multiplicity approach [Dori95, Dori02, Dori16], respectively picks a model for each view as shown in Figure 1-7, the structure view has the structure model; the behavior view has the behavior model; the function view has the function model; the data view has the data model. These multiple models, are heterogeneous and not related to each other, and thus become the primary cause of model multiplicity problems [Dori95, Dori02, Dori16, Pele02, Sode03].

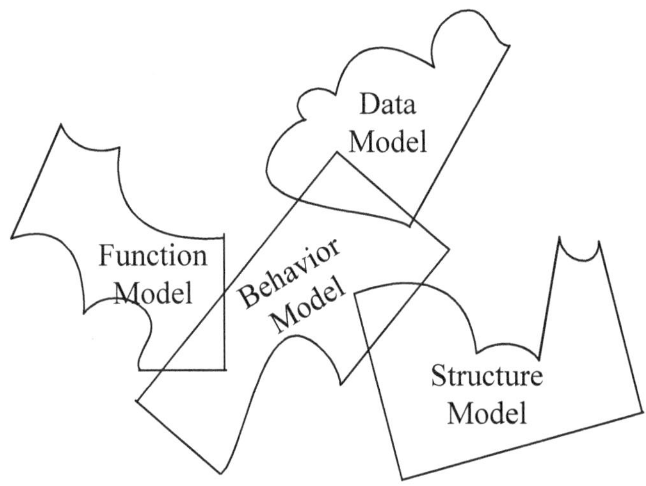

Figure 1-7 Multiple Views Non-Integrated Approach

Multiple views non-integrated approaches for program design 1.0 fall into three general categories: data-oriented, function-oriented and object-oriented [Grad13, Hatl00], as shown in Figure 1-8. Each of these approaches, more or less, fails to describe a software system as an integrated whole of that software system's multiple views.

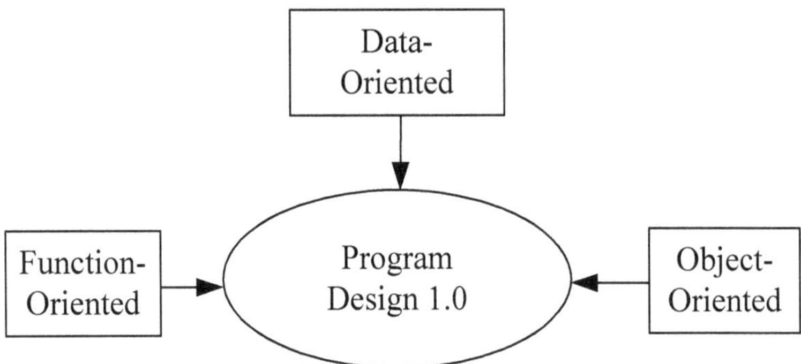

Figure 1-8 Multiple Views Non-Integrated Approaches for Program Design 1.0

Data-oriented approaches for program design 1.0 stress the software system state as a data structure. Jackson System Development (JSD) [Came89] and Entity Relationship Modeling (ERM) [Chen76] are primarily data-oriented. Data-oriented approaches concentrate only on data and completely neglect to integrate the software structure and software behavior. Therefore, data-oriented approaches are multiple views non-integrated and will never become an ideal program design approach.

Function-oriented approaches for program design 1.0 take the primary view of the way a software system transforms input data into output data. Each transformation from input data into output data demonstrates a function of the software system. A software system may contain many such kinds of functions which represent the function view of the software system. Classical Structured Analysis (SA) [DeMa79] fits into the category of function-oriented approaches, as do Structured Analysis and Design Technique (SADT) [Marc88] and Structured Systems Analysis and Design Method (SSADM) [Ashw90]. Function-oriented approaches concentrate only on the function view and completely neglect to integrate the software structure and software behavior. Just like data-oriented approaches, function-oriented approaches are multiple views non-integrated and will never become an ideal program design approach.

Object-oriented approaches for program design 1.0 design the software system as classes of objects and their behaviors. Object-oriented Design (OOD) [Booc07], fitting into the category of object-oriented methods. Object-oriented approaches stress both the structure view and the behavior view, but not an integrated structure and behavior views. Object-oriented approaches do not emphasize to integrate the software structure and software behavior. Like data-oriented and function-oriented approaches, object-oriented approaches are multiple views non-integrated and will never become an ideal program design approach.

1-5 Multiple Views Integrated Approaches for Program Design 2.0

When designing a software system, the multiple views integrated approach, also known as the model singularity approach [Dori95, Dori02, Dori16, Pele02, Sode03], instead of picking many heterogeneous and unrelated models, will use only one single model as shown in Figure 1-9. The structure, behavior, function and data views are all integrated in this one single model which represents an integrated whole of that system's multiple views [Chao14a, Chao14b, Chao14c].

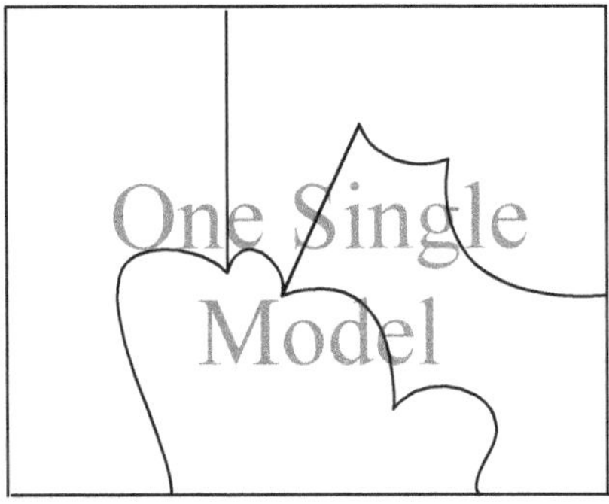

Figure 1-9 Multiple Views Integrated Approach

Multiple views integrated approaches for program design 2.0 design a software system as an integrated whole of that software's multiple views.

Chapter 2: Software Structure and Software Behavior

Software structure and software behavior are the two most significant views of a software system. Software structure, designed by components, their operations and their composition, refers to the type of connection between the components of a software system. Software behavior, designed by the interactions between and among the components and environment, refers to the interconnectivities a software system in conjunction with its environment.

2-1 Software Structure

Every software system forms a whole. In general, software structure is the type of connection between the components of a software system. More specifically, we design the software structure by 1) components, 2) their operations and 3) their composition.

Components are something relatively indivisible in a software system [Hoff10, Shel11]. For example, *MTPDS_GUI*, *Age_Logic*, *Overweight_Logic* and *Personal_Database* are components of the *Multi-Tier Personal Data System* as shown in Figure 2-1.

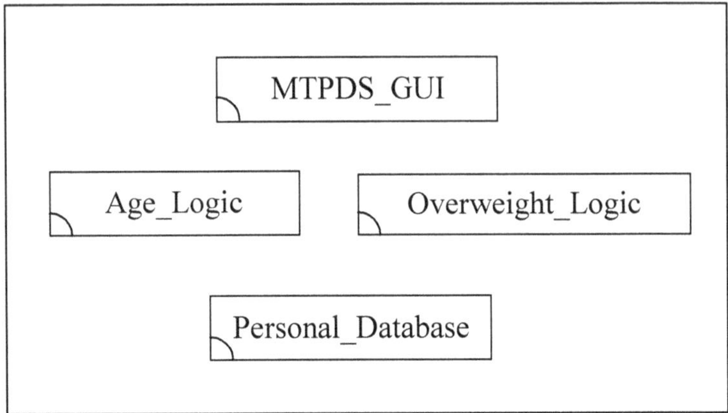

Figure 2-1 Components of
the *Multi-Tier Personal Data System*

An operation provided by each component represents a procedure or method or function of the component [Chao14a, Chao14b, Chao14c]. Each component in a software system must possess at least one operation. Figure 2-2 shows the operations of all components of the *Multi-Tier Personal Data System*. In the figure, component *MTPDS_GUI* has two operations: *Calculate_AgeClick* and *Calculate_OverweightClick*; component *Age_Logic* has one operation: *Calculate_Age*; component *Overweight_Logic* has one operation: *Calculate_Overweight*; component *Personal_Database* has two operations: *Sql_DateOfBirth_Select* and *Sql_SexHeightWeight_Select*.

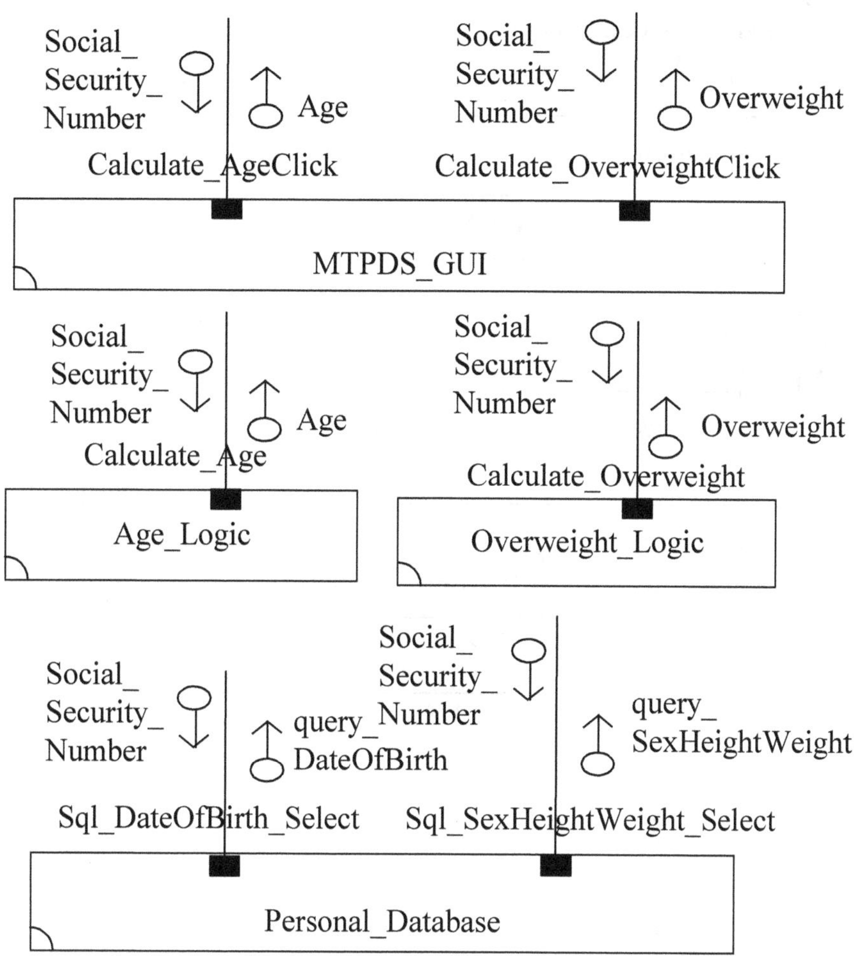

Figure 2-2 Operations of all Components of the *Multi-Tier Personal Data System*

Composition of components designs the structural composition and decomposition of a software system. For example, Figure 2-3 shows that, in the *Multi-Tier Personal Data System*, *Presentation_Layer* contains the *MTPDS_GUI* component; *Logic_Layer* contains the *Age_Logic* and

Overweight_Logic components; *Data_Layer* contains the *Personal_Database* component.

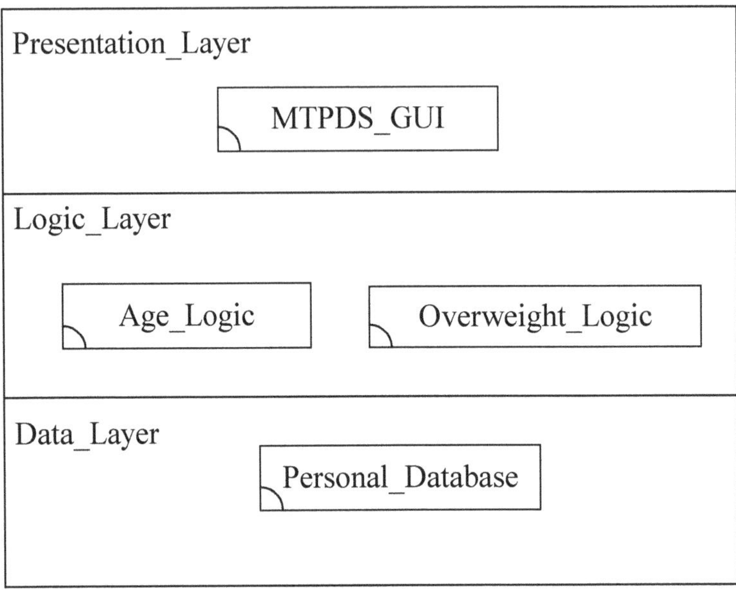

Figure 2-3 Structural Composition of the *Multi-Tier Personal Data System*

2-2 Software Behavior

Software behavior refers to the interactions a software system in conjunction with its environment. It is the response of a software system to various stimuli, whether internal or external, conscious or subconscious, overt or covert, and voluntary or involuntary.

For example, Figure 2-4 demonstrates two individual behaviors: *AgeCalculation* and *OverweightCalculation* that refer to the interactions the *Multi-Tier Personal Data System* in conjunction with its environment.

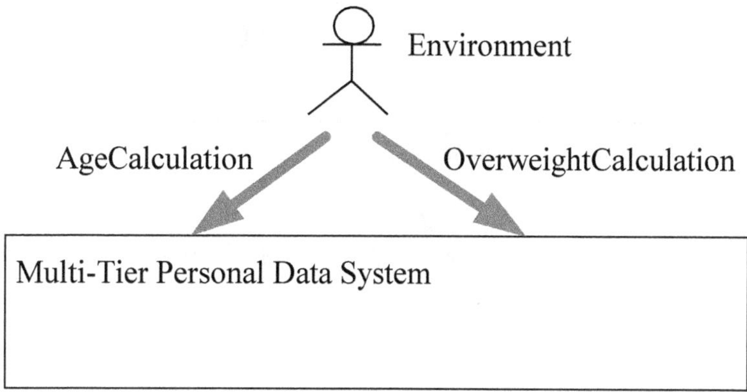

Figure 2-4 Behaviors of
the *Multi-Tier Personal Data System*

For each behavior, the environment always initiates the interaction and will lead more follow-up interactions to be realized among components. For example, Figure 2-5 demonstrates that interactions between and among the environment and the *MTPDS_GUI*, *Age_Logic* and *Personal_Database* components shall draw forth the *AgeCalculation* behavior.

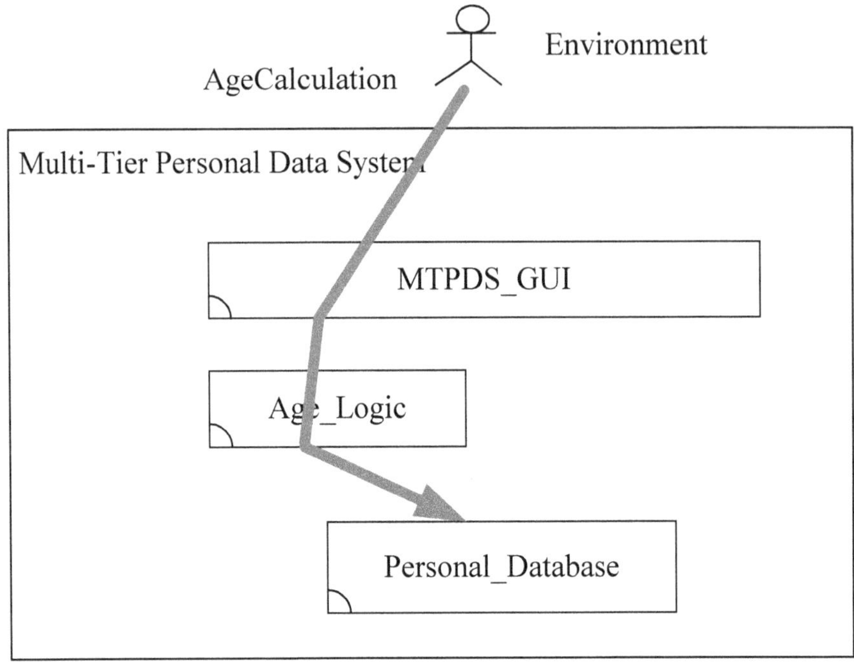

Figure 2-5 Interactions that Draw forth the *AgeCalculation* Behavior

As a second example, Figure 2-6 demonstrates that interactions between and among the environment and the *MTPDS_GUI*, *Overweight_Logic* and *Personal_Database* components shall draw forth the *OverweightCalculation* behavior.

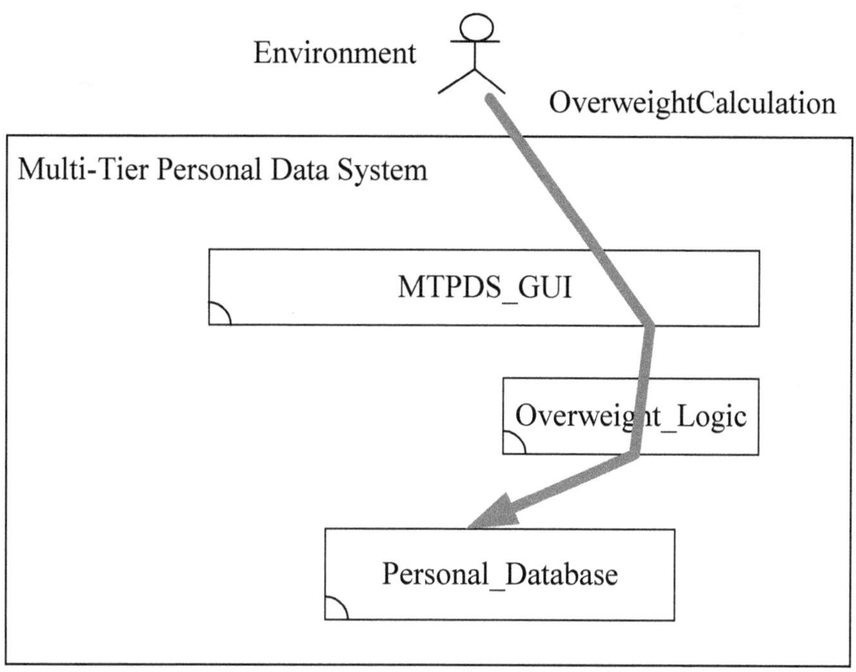

Figure 2-6 Interactions that Draw forth the *OverweightCalculation* Behavior

Chapter 3: Structure-Behavior Coalescence

A software system has been designed hopefully to be an integrated whole, embodied in its assembled components, their interactions with each other and the environment. Since software structure and software behavior are the two most prominent views of a software system, integrating them apparently is the best way to achieve a truly integrated whole of a software system. Because program design 1.0 does not specify the integration of software structure and software behavior, very likely it will never be able to actually form an integrated whole of a software system.

Structure-behavior coalescence (SBC) provides an elegant way to integrate the software structure and software behavior, and hence achieves a truly integrated whole, of a software system. A truly integrated whole sets a path to achieve the desired program design. SBC facilitates an integrated whole. Therefore, we conclude that SBC sets a path to achieve the program design. Program design 2.0 uses the SBC approach and is highly adequate in designing a software system.

3-1 Integrated Whole to Achieve the Program Design

A software system has been designed hopefully to be an integrated whole, embodied in its assembled components, their interactions with each other and the environment. In other words, an integrated whole sets a path to achieve the program design as shown in Figure 3-1.

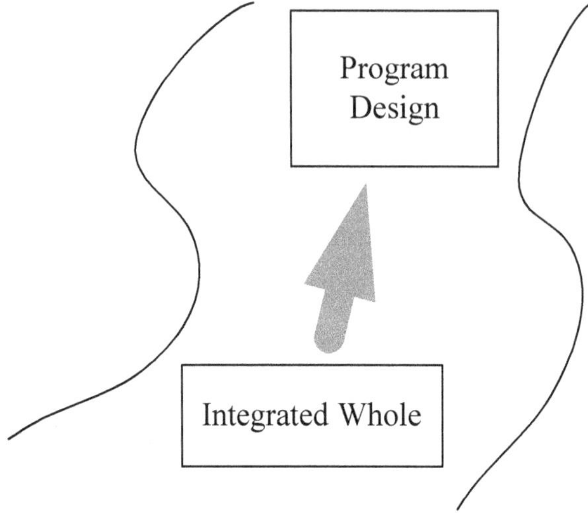

Figure 3-1 Integrated Whole to Achieve the Program Design

In one program design, different software structures may draw forth the same integrated whole as shown in Figure 3-2.

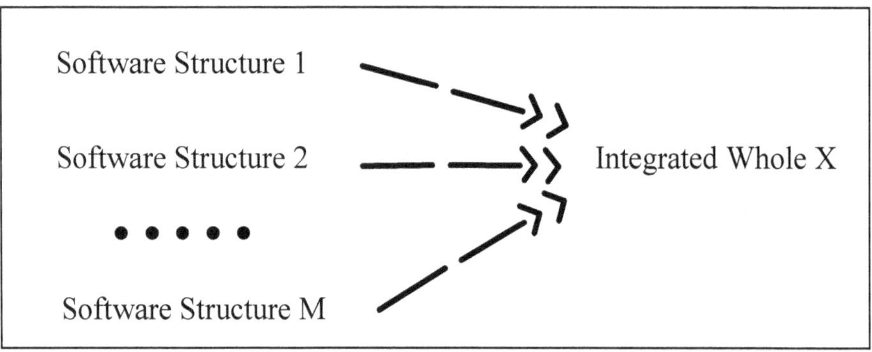

Figure 3-2 Different Software Structures Draw Forth the Same Integrated Whole

Since there is only one software structure exists in one program design, one software structure will draw forth one integrated whole as shown in Figure 3-3.

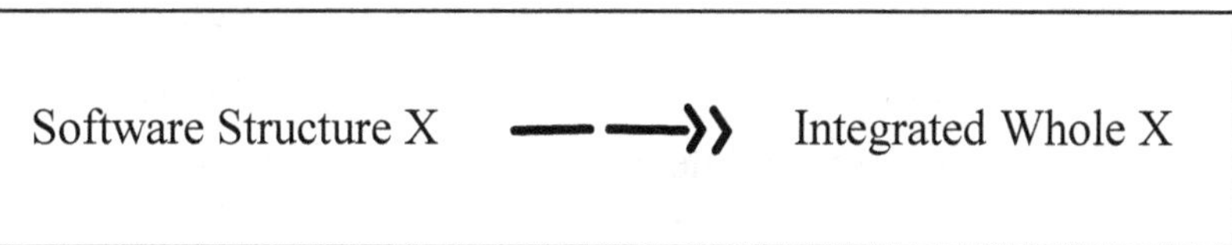

Figure 3-3 One Software Structure Draws Forth One Integrated Whole

We conclude that in one program design, an integrated whole must be attached to or built on a software structure. In other words, an integrated whole shall not exist alone; it must be loaded on a software structure just like a cargo is loaded on a ship as shown in Figure 3-4. There will be no integrated whole if there is no software structure. A stand-alone integrated whole with no software structure is not meaningful.

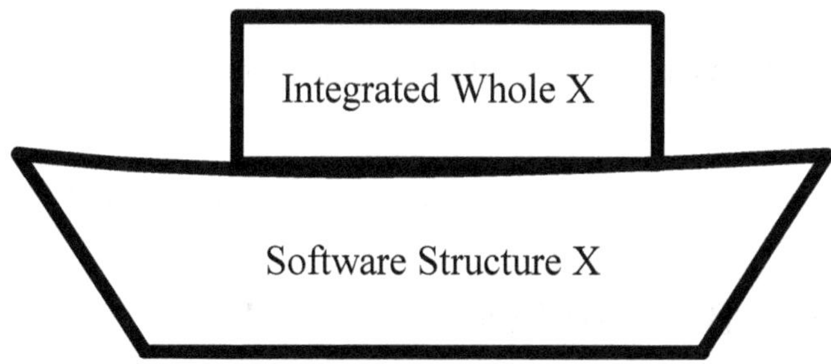

Figure 3-4 An Integrated Whole Must be Loaded on a Software Structure

3-2 Integrating the Software Structure and Software Behavior

By integrating the software structures and software behaviors, we obtain structure-behavior coalescence (SBC) within a software system. Since software structures and software behaviors are so tightly integrated, we sometimes claim that the core theme of structure-behavior coalescence is: "Software Architecture = Software Structure + Software Behavior," as shown in Figure 3-5.

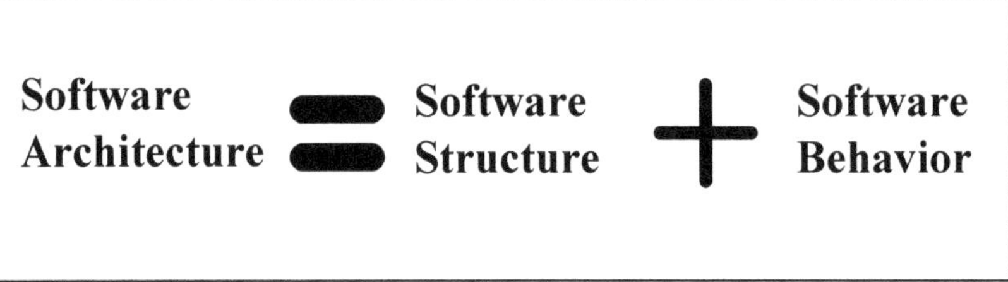

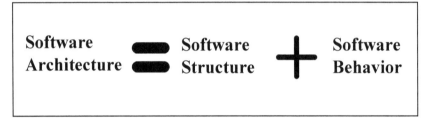

Figure 3-5 Core Theme of Structure-Behavior Coalescence

So far, integrating the software structure and software behavior has never been proposed or suggested besides the SBC approach. In most cases, software behaviors are separated from software structures when designing a software system [Hoff10, Pres09, Shel11, Somm06].

3-3 Structure-Behavior Coalescence to Facilitate an Integrated Whole

Since software structure and software behavior are the two most prominent views of a software system, integrating them apparently is the best way to achieve a truly integrated whole of a software system. If we are not able to integrate the software structure and software behavior, then there is no way that we are able to integrate the whole software system. In other words, structure-behavior coalescence (SBC) facilitates a truly integrated whole as shown in Figure 3-6.

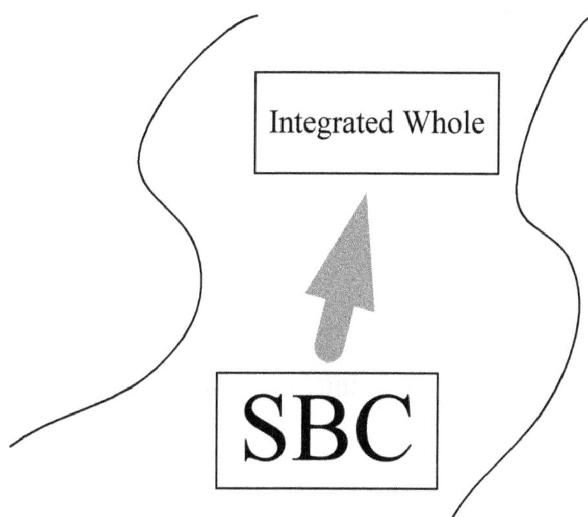

Figure 3-6 SBC Facilitates an Integrated Whole

Since program design 1.0 does not design the integration of software structure and software behavior, very likely it will never be able to actually form an integrated whole of a software system. In this situation, program design 1.0 is powerless in designing a software system adequately.

3-4 Structure-Behavior Coalescence to Achieve the Program Design

Figure 3-1 declares that an integrated whole sets a path to achieve the desired program design. Figure 3-6 declares that structure-behavior coalescence facilitates a truly integrated whole.

Combining the above two declarations, we conclude that the structure-behavior coalescence (SBC) approach sets a path to achieve the program design as shown in Figure 3-7.

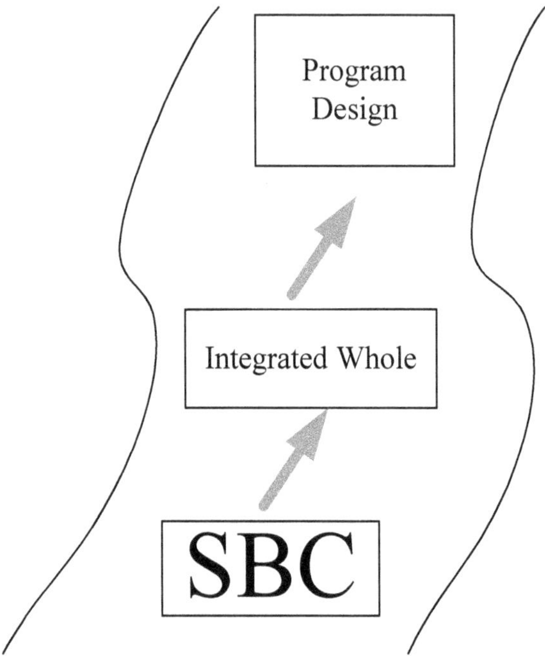

Figure 3-7 SBC to Achieve the Program Design

In the SBC approach, different software structures may draw forth the same software behavior as shown in Figure 3-8.

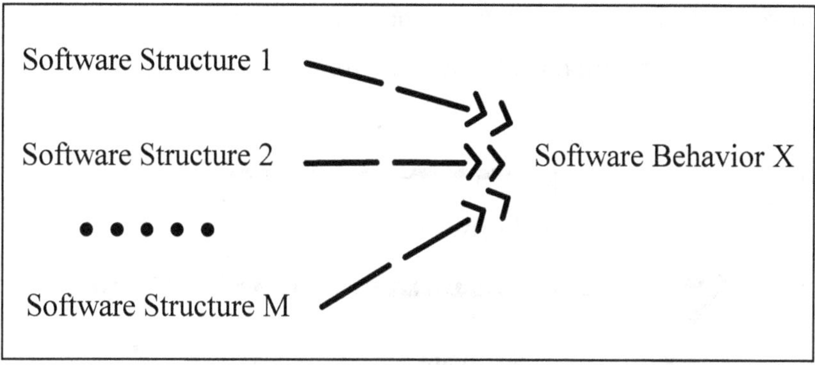

Figure 3-8 Different Software Structures Draw Forth the Same Software Behavior

Since there is only one software structure exists in one program design, one software behavior will always be attached to or built on one software structure as shown in Figure 3-9.

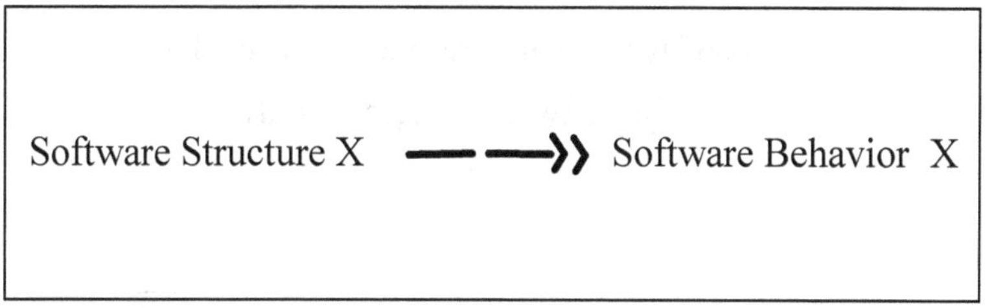

Software Structure X ——» Software Behavior X

Figure 3-9 One Software Behavior is Attached to One Software Structure

We conclude that in the SBC approach, a software behavior must be attached to or built on a software structure. In other words, a software behavior can not exist alone; it must be loaded on a software structure just like a cargo is loaded on a ship as shown in Figure 3-10. There will be no software behavior if there is no software structure. A stand-alone software behavior with no software structure is not meaningful.

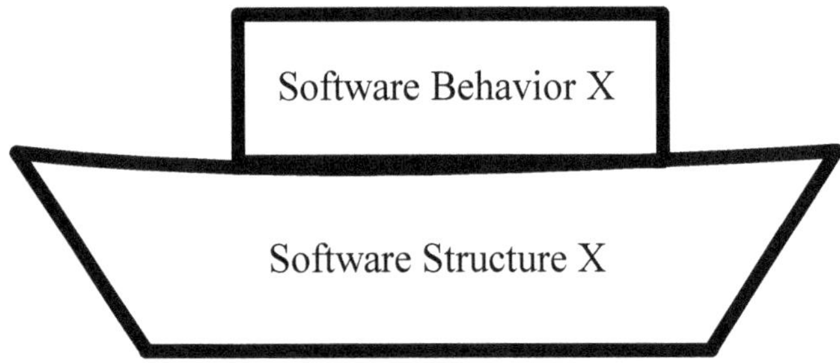

Figure 3-10 A Software Behavior Must be Loaded on a Software Structure

3-5 SBC Approach for Program Design 2.0

Since structure-behavior coalescence (SBC) provides an elegant way to integrate the software structure and software behavior, we shall include it in the design of a software system. Figure 3-11 shows how the program design 2.0 designs a software system.

A software system, through the SBC approach, truly is an integrated whole, embodied in its assembled components, their interactions with each other and the environment.

Figure 3-11 Program Design 2.0 Designing a Software System

A software system designed by the program design 2.0 has the following characteristics: 1) it emphasizes the software system's structure-behavior coalescence; 2) it is a truly integrated whole; 3) it is embodied in its assembled components; 4) components are interacting (or handshaking) [Chao15a, Chao15b, Chao15c, Chao15d, Chao15e, Hoar85, Miln89, Miln99] with each other and the environment; and 5) it uses structural decomposition [Chao14a, Chao14b, Chao14c, Ghar11] rather than functional decomposition [Scho10].

Structure-behavior coalescence (SBC) provides an elegant way to integrate the software structure and software behavior of a software system. Program design 2.0 uses the SBC approach to formally design the integration of software structure and software behavior of a software system. Program design 2.0 contains three fundamental diagrams: a) framework diagram, b) component operation diagram and c) interaction flow diagram.

So far, we have introduced the program design 2.0 which should be able to appropriately design a software system. In the following chapters, we shall elaborate the details of the program design 2.0.

3-6 SBC Model Singularity

Channel-Based Single-Queue SBC Process Algebra (C-S-SBC-PA) [Chao17a], Channel-Based Multi-Queue SBC Process Algebra (C-M-SBC-PA) [Chao17b], Channel-Based Infinite-Queue SBC Process Algebra (C-I-SBC-PA) [Chao17c], Operation-Based Single-Queue SBC Process Algebra (O-S-SBC-PA) [Chao17d], Operation-Based Multi-Queue SBC Process Algebra (O-M-SBC-PA) [Chao17e] and Operation-Based Infinite-Queue SBC Process Algebra (O-I-SBC-PA) [Chao17f] are the six specialized SBC process algebras. The SBC process algebra (SBC-PA) shown in Figure 3-12 is a model singularity approach.

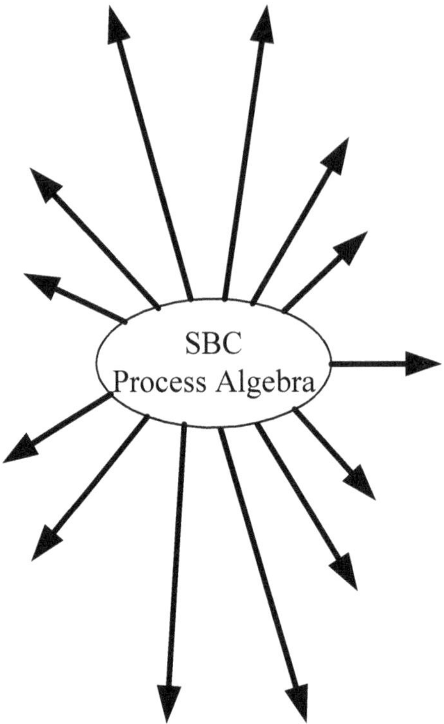

Figure 3-12 SBC-PA is a Model Singularity Approach.

The program design 2.0 is also a model singularity approach. With SBC mind set sitting in the kernel, the program design 2.0 single model shown in Figure 3-13 is therefore able to represent all structural views such as framework diagram (FD), component operation diagram (COD), and behavioral views such as interaction flow diagram (IFD).

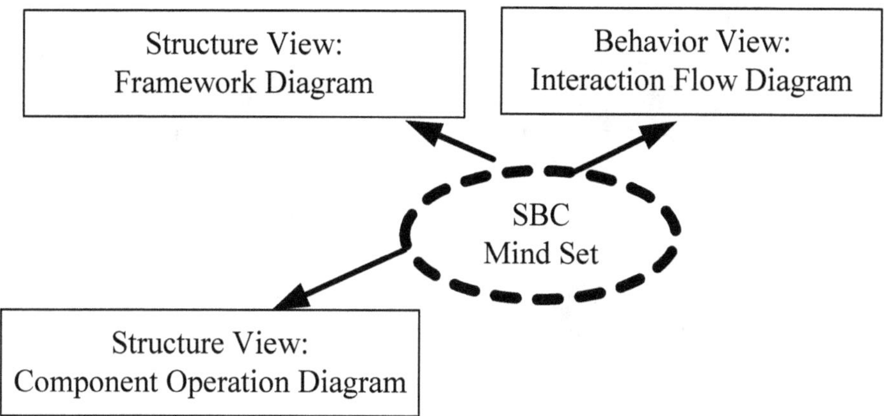

Figure 3-13 Program Design 2.0 is a Model Singularity Approach.

The combination of SBC process algebra (SBC-PA) and program design 2.0 is shown in Figure 3-14, again as a model singularity approach.

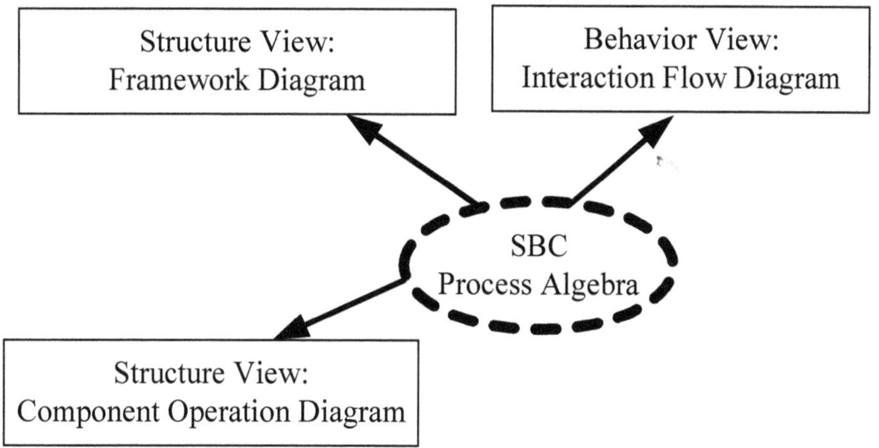

Figure 3-14 SBC Model is a Model Singularity Approach.

PART II: SBC APPROACH FOR PROGRAM DESIGN 2.0

Chapter 4: Framework Diagram

SBC approach for program design 2.0 uses a framework diagram (FD) to design the multi-layer (also referred to as multi-tier) decomposition and composition of a software system.

4-1 Multi-Layer Decomposition and Composition

Decomposition and composition of a software system can be designed in a multi-layer manner. We draw a framework diagram (FD) for the multi-layer decomposition and composition of a software system.

As the first example, Figure 4-1 shows a FD of the *Multi-Tier Personal Data System*. In the figure, *Presentation_Layer* contains the *MTPDS_GUI* component; *Logic_Layer* contains the *Age_Logic* and *Overweight_Logic* components; *Data_Layer* contains the *Personal_Database* component.

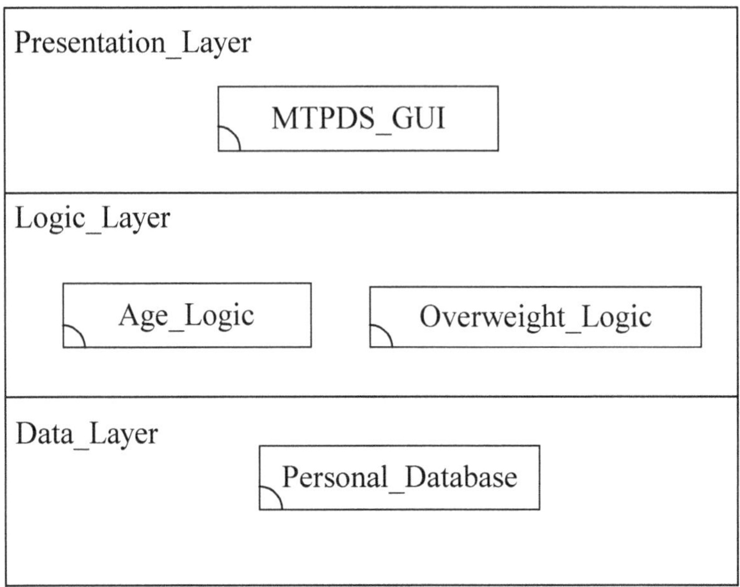

Figure 4-1 FD of the *Multi-Tier Personal Data System*

As the second example, Figure 4-2 shows a FD of the *Unix-Like Operating System*. In the figure, *Server_Layer* contains the *Memory_Manager* and *File_Manager* components; *Device_Driver_Layer* contains the *Terminal_Manager* and *Disk_Manager* components; *CPU_Layer* contains the *CPU_Manager* component.

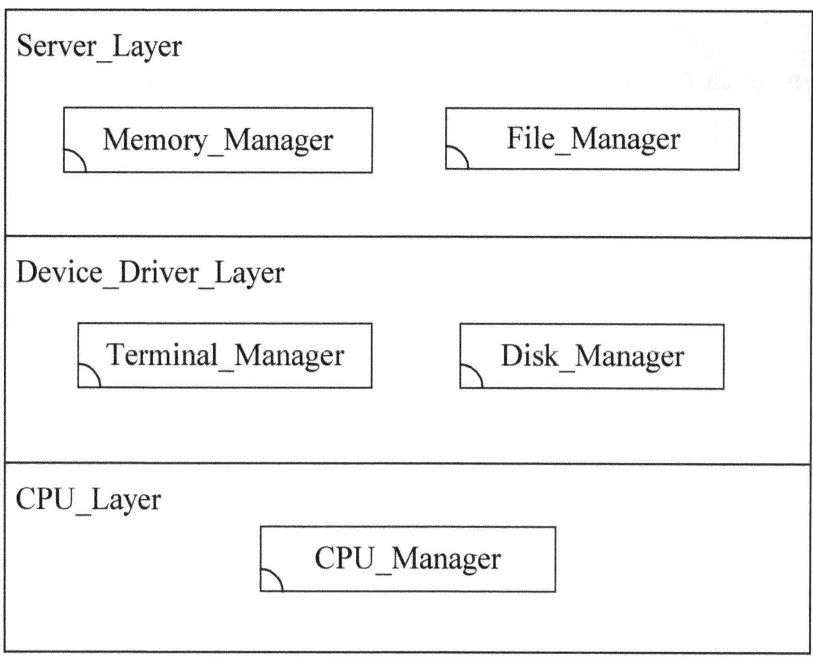

Figure 4-2 FD of the *Unix-Like Operating System*

4-2 Only Non-Aggregated Systems Appearing in Framework Diagrams

It is interesting that we see only non-aggregated systems shall appear in the multi-layer FD decomposition and composition of a software system.

For the first example, Figure 4-1 in the previous section shows a FD of the *Multi-Tier Personal Data System* in which only non-aggregated systems such as *MTPDS_GUI*, *Age_Logic*, *Overweight_Logic* and *Personal_Database* are displayed.

For a second example, Figure 4-2 in the previous section shows a FD of the *Unix-Like Operating System* in which only non-aggregated systems such as *Memory_Manager*, *File_Manager*, *Terminal_Manager*, *Disk_Manager* and *CPU_Manager* are displayed.

Chapter 5: Component Operation Diagram

SBC approach for program design 2.0 uses a component operation diagram (COD) to design all components' operations of a software system.

5-1 Operations of Each Component

An operation provided by each component represents a procedure or method or function of the component. If other components request this component to perform an operation, then shall use it to accomplish the operation request.

Each component in a software system must possess at least one operation. A component should not exist in a software system if it does not possess any operation. Figure 5-1 shows that the *MTPDS_GUI* component has two operations: *Calculate_AgeClick* and *Calculate_OverweightClick*.

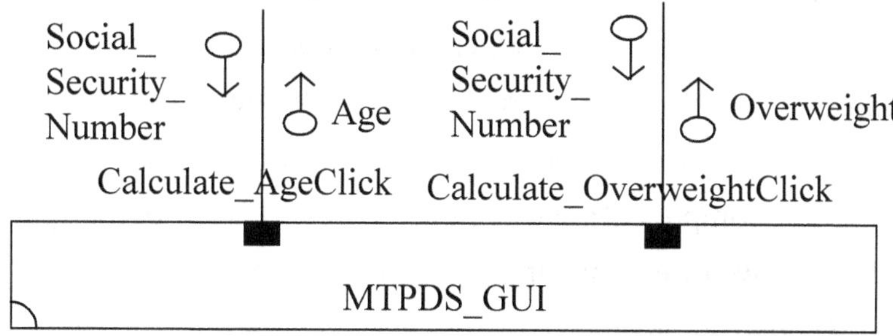

Figure 5-1 Two Operations of the *MTPDS_GUI* Component

An operation formula is utilized to fully represent an operation. An operation formula includes a) operation name, b) input parameters and c) output parameters as shown in Figure 5-2.

Operation_Name (In $i_1, i_2, \ldots, i_m$; Out $o_1, o_2, \ldots, o_n$)

Figure 5-2 Operation Formula

Operation name is the name of this operation. In a software system, every operation name should be unique. Duplicate operation names shall not be allowed in any software system.

An operation may have several input and output parameters. The input and output parameters, gathered from all operations, represent the input data and output data views of a software system [Date03, Elma10]. As shown in Figure 5-3, component *Personal_Database* possesses the *Sql_DateOfBirth_Select* operation which has the *Social_Security_Number* input parameter (with the arrow direction pointing to the component) and the *query_DateOfBirth* output parameter (with the arrow direction opposite to the component); component *Personal_Database* also possesses the *Sql_SexHeightWeight_Select* operation which has the *Social_Security_Number* input parameter (with the arrow direction pointing to the component) and the *query_SexHeightWeight* output parameter (with the arrow direction opposite to the component).

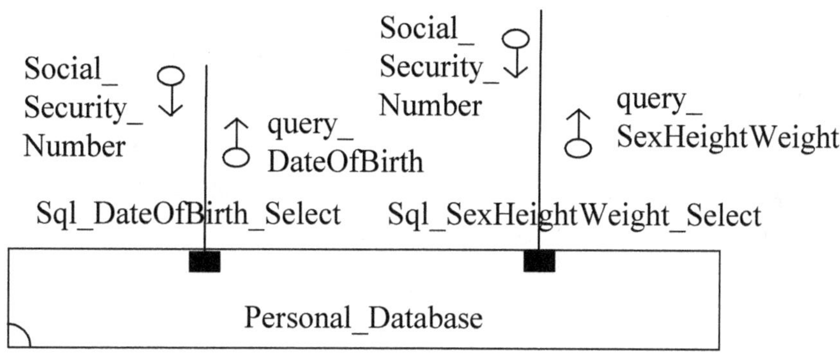

Figure 5-3 Input/Output Parameters

Data formats of input and output parameters can be described by data type specifications. There are two sets of data types: primitive and composite [Date03, Elma10]. Figure 5-4 shows the primitive data type specification of the *Social_Security_Number* input parameter occurring in the *Sql_DateOfBirth_Select(In Social_Security_Number; Out query_DateOfBirth)* operation formula.

Parameter	Data Type	Instances
Social_Security_Number	Text	424-87-3651

Figure 5-4 Primitive Data Type Specification

Figure 5-5 shows the composite data type specification of the *query_DateOfBirth* output parameter occurring in the *Sql_DateOfBirth_Select(In Social_Security_Number; Out query_DateOfBirth)* operation formula.

Parameter	*query_DateOfBirth*
Data Type	TABLE of Social_Security_Number : Text Age : Integer End TABLE;
Instances	424-87-3651 | 28 512-24-3722 | 56

Figure 5-5 Composite Data Type Specification of *query_DateOfBirth*

Figure 5-6 shows the composite data type specification of the *query_SexHeightWeight* output parameter occurring in the *Sql_SexHeightWeight_Select(In Social_Security_Number; Out query_SexHeightWeight)* operation formula.

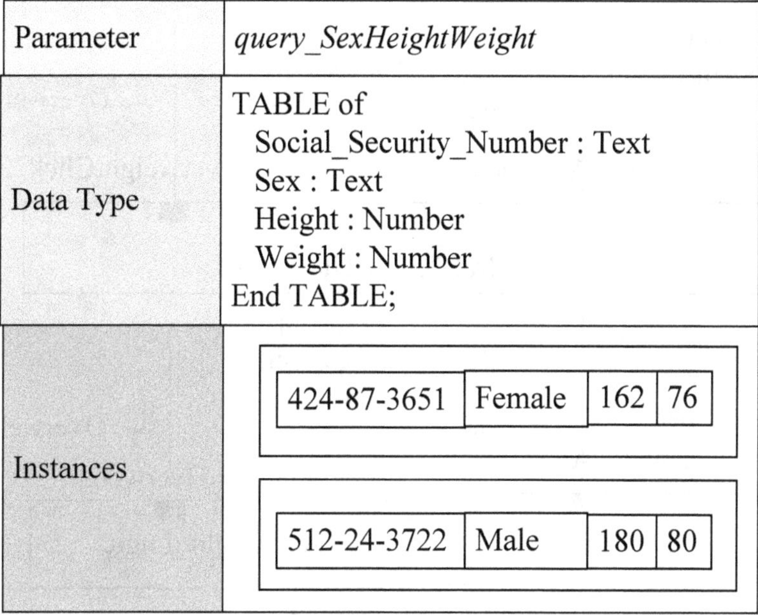

Parameter	*query_SexHeightWeight*
Data Type	TABLE of Social_Security_Number : Text Sex : Text Height : Number Weight : Number End TABLE;
Instances	424-87-3651 | Female | 162 | 76 512-24-3722 | Male | 180 | 80

Figure 5-6 Composite Data Type Specification of *query_SexHeightWeight*

5-2 Drawing the Component Operation Diagram

For a software system, COD is used to design all components' operations. Figure 5-7 shows the *Multi-Tier Personal Data System's COD*. In the figure, component *MTPDS_GUI* has two operations: *Calculate_AgeClick* and *Calculate_OverweightClick*; component *Age_Logic* has one operation: *Calculate_Age*; component *Overweight_Logic* has one operation: *Calculate_Overweight*; component *Personal_Database* has two operations: *Sql_DateOfBirth_Select* and *Sql_SexHeightWeight_Select*.

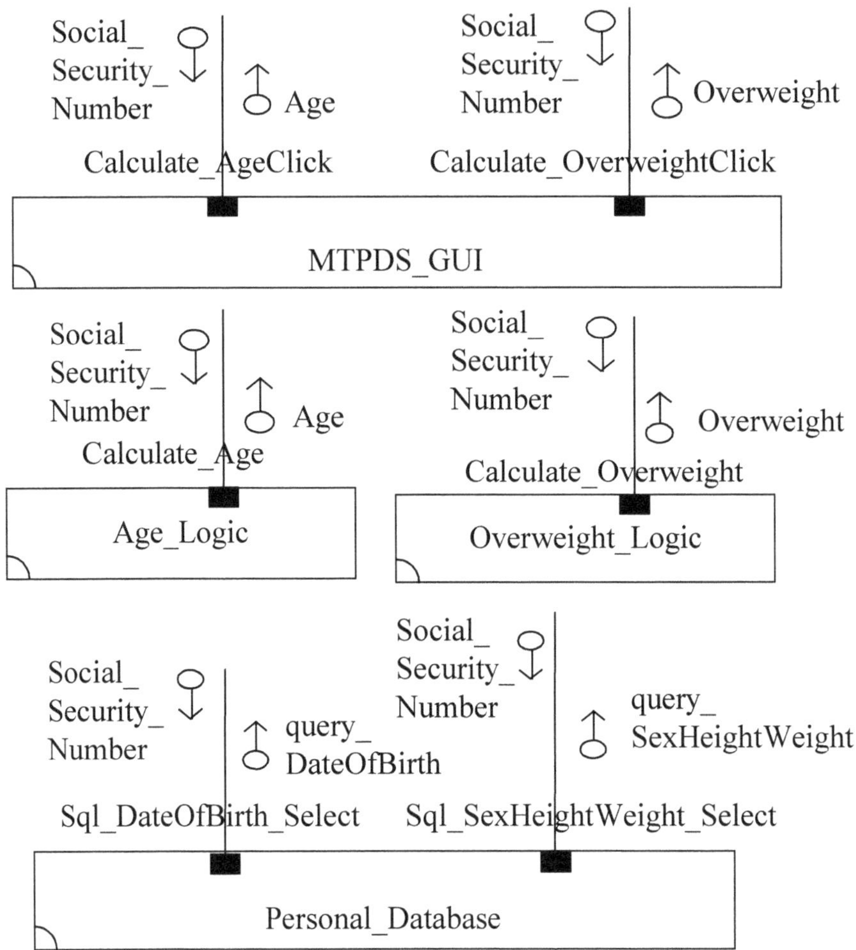

Figure 5-7 COD of the *Multi-Tier Personal Data System*

Chapter 6: Interaction Flow Diagram

SBC approach for program design 2.0 uses an interaction flow diagram (IFD) to design each individual behavior of the overall behavior of a software system.

6-1 Individual Behavior Represented by Interaction Flow Diagram

The overall behavior of a software system consists of many individual behaviors. Each individual behavior represents an execution path. An IFD is used to design such an individual behavior.

Figure 6-1 demonstrates that the *Multi-Tier Personal Data System* has two behaviors; thus, it has two IFDs.

System	IFD
Multi-Tier Personal Data System	AgeCalculation
	OverweightCalculation

Figure 6-1 *Multi-Tier Personal Data System* has Two IFDs

Figure 6-2 demonstrates that the *Unix-Like Operating System* has five behaviors; thus, it has five IFDs.

System	IFD
Unix-Like Operating System	Login
	ForkProcess
	ProcessExit
	ReadFromFile
	WriteIntoFile

Figure 6-2 *Unix-Like Operating System* has Five IFDs

6-2 Drawing the Interaction Flow Diagram

Let us now explain the usage of interaction flow diagram (IFD) by drawing an IFD step by step. Figure 6-3 demonstrates an IFD of the *AgeCalculation* behavior. The X-axis direction is from the left side to right side and the Y-axis direction is from the above to the below. Inside an IFD, there are four elements: a) external environment's actor, b) components, c) interactions and d) input/output parameters. Participants of the interaction, such as the external environment's actor and each component, are laid aside along the X-axis direction on the top of the diagram. The external environment's actor which initiates the sequential interactions is always placed on the most left side of the X-axis. Then, interactions among the external environment's actor and components successively in turn decorate along the Y-axis direction. The first interaction is placed on the top of the Y-axis position. The last interaction is placed on the bottom of the Y-axis position. Each interaction may carry several input and/or output parameters.

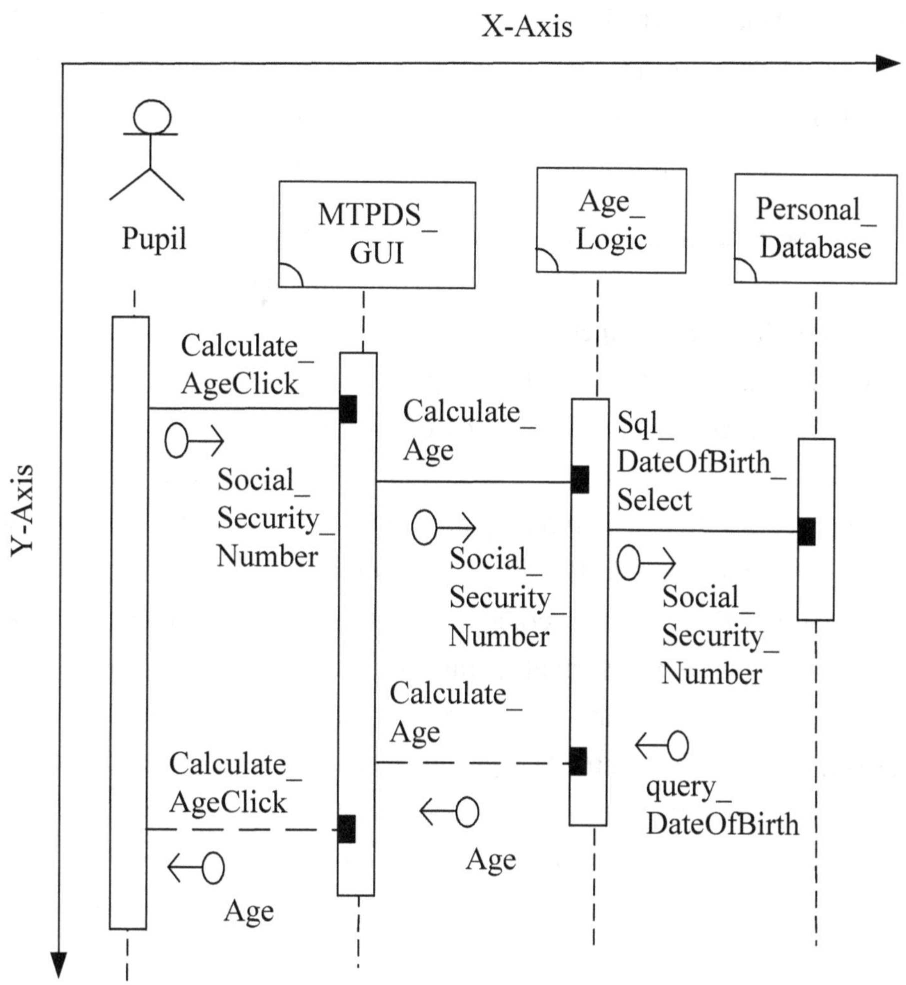

Figure 6-3 IFD of the *AgeCalculation* Behavior

In Figure 6-3, *Pupil* is an external environment's actor. *MTPDS_GUI*, *Age_Logic* and *Personal_Database* are components. *Calculate_AgeClick* is an operation, carrying the

Social_Security_Number input parameter and *Age* output parameter, which is provided by the *MTPDS_GUI* component. *Calculate_Age* is an operation, carrying the *Social_Security_Number* input parameter and *Age* output parameter, which is provided by the *Age_Logic* component, *Sql_DateOfBirth_Select* is an operation, carrying the *Social_Security_Number* input parameter and *query_DateOfBirth* output parameter, which is provided by the *Personal_Database* component.

The execution path of Figure 6-3 is as follows. First, actor *Pupil* interacts with the *MTPDS_GUI* component through the *Calculate_AgeClick* operation call interaction, carrying the *Social_Security_Number* input parameter. Next, component *MTPDS_GUI* interacts with the *AgeCalculation* component through the *Calculate_Age* operation call interaction, carrying the *Social_Security_Number* input parameter. Continuingly, component *Age_Logic* interacts with the *Personal_Database* component through the *Sql_DateOfBirth_Select* operation call interaction, carrying the *Social_Security_Number* input parameter and the *query_DateOfBirth* output parameter. Repeatedly, component *MTPDS_GUI* interacts with the *Age_Logic* component through the *Calculate_Age* operation return interaction, carrying the *Age* output parameter. Finally, actor *Pupil* interacts with the *MTPDS_GUI* component through the *Calculate_AgeClick* operation return interaction, carrying the *Age* output parameter.

For each interaction, the solid line stands for operation call while the dashed line stands for operation return. The operation call and operation return interactions, if using the same operation name, belong to the identical operation. Figure 6-4 exhibits two interactions (operation call interaction and operation return interaction) having the identical "*Calculate_OverweightClick*" operation.

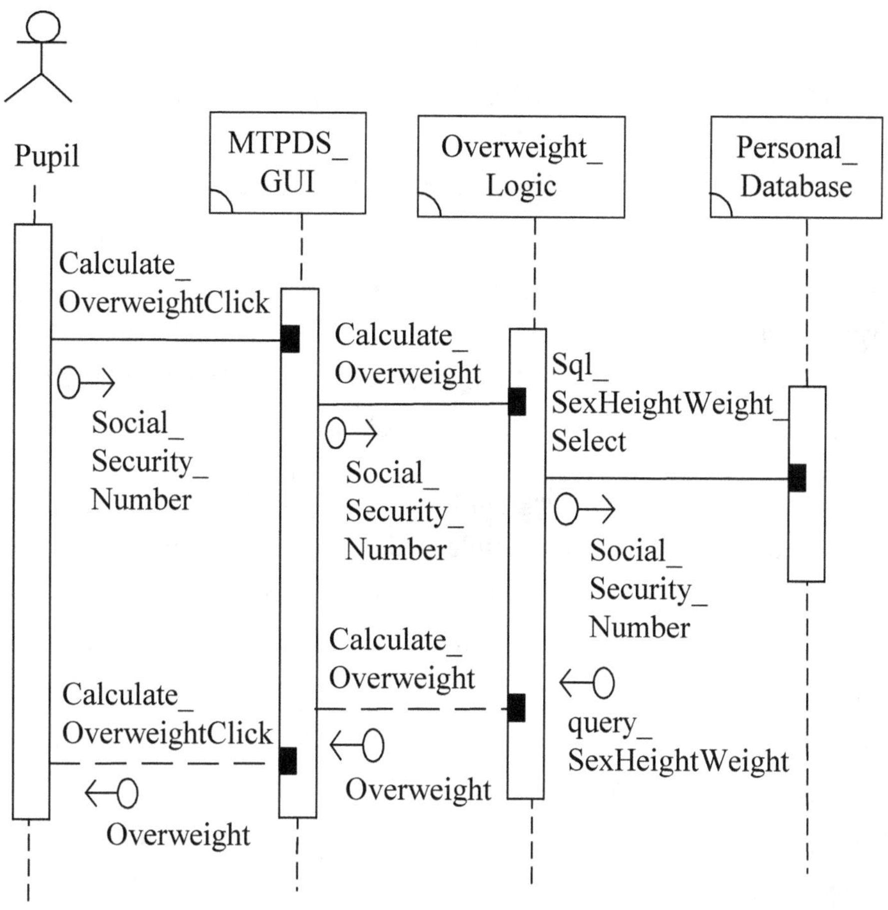

Figure 6-4 Two Interactions Have the Identical Operation

The execution path of Figure 6-4 is as follows. First, actor *Pupil* interacts with the *MTPDS_GUI* component through the *Calculate_OverweightClick* operation call interaction, carrying the *Social_Security_Number* input parameter. Next, component *MTPDS_GUI* interacts with the *OverweightCalculation* component through the *Calculate_Overweight* operation call interaction, carrying the

Social_Security_Number input parameter. Continuingly, component *Overweight_Logic* interacts with the *Personal_Database* component through the *Sql_SexHeightWeight_Select* operation call interaction, carrying the *Social_Security_Number* input parameter and the *query_SexHeightWeight* output parameter. Repeatedly, component *MTPDS_GUI* interacts with the *Overweight_Logic* component through the *Calculate_Overweight* operation return interaction, carrying the *Overweight* output parameter. Finally, actor *Pupil* interacts with the *MTPDS_GUI* component through the *Calculate_OverweightClick* operation return interaction, carrying the *Overweight* output parameter.

An interaction flow diagram may contain a conditional expression. Figure 6-5 shows such an example which has the following execution path. First, external environment's actor *Employee* interacts with the *Computer* component through the *Open* operation call interaction, carrying the *Task_No* input parameter. Next, if the *var_1 < 4 & var_2 > 7* condition is true then component *Computer* shall interact with the *Skype* component through the *Op_1* operation call interaction and component *Skype* shall interact with the *Earphone* component through the *Op_4* operation call interaction, carrying the *Skype_Earphone* output parameter; else if the *var_3 = 99* condition is true then component *Computer* shall interact with the *Skype* component through the *Op_2* operation call interaction and component *Skype* shall interact with the *Speaker* component through the *Op_5* operation call interaction, carrying the *Skype_Speaker* output parameter; else component *Computer* shall interact with the *Youtube* component through the *Op_3* operation call interaction and component *Youtube* shall interact with the *Speaker* component through the *Op_6* operation call interaction, carrying the *Youtube_Speaker* output parameter. Continuingly, if the *var_1 < 4 & var_2 > 7* condition is true then component *Computer* shall interact with the *Skype* component through the *Op_1* operation return interaction, carrying the *Status_1* output parameter; else if the *var_3 = 99* condition is true then component *Computer* shall interact with the *Skype* component through the *Op_2* operation return interaction, carrying the *Status_2* output parameter; else component *Computer* shall interact with the *Youtube* component through the *Op_3* operation return interaction, carrying the *Status_3* output parameter. Finally, external environment's actor *Employee* interacts with the *Computer* component through the *Open* operation return interaction, carrying the *Status* output parameter.

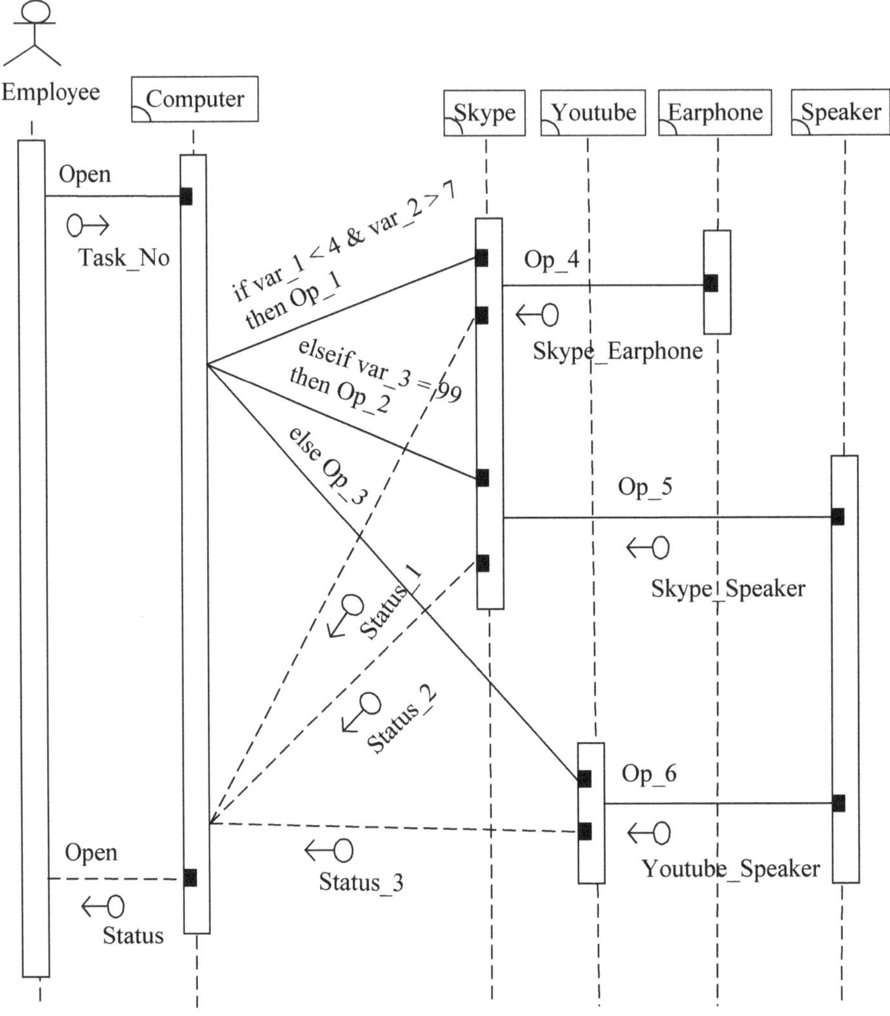

Figure 6-5 Conditional Interaction

Several Boolean conditions are shown in Figure 6-5. They are "*var_1 < 4 & var_2 > 7*" and "*var_3 = 99*". Variables, such as *var_1*, *var_2* and *var_3*, appearing in the Boolean condition can be local or global variables [Prat00, Seth96].

PART III: CASES STUDY

Chapter 7: Program Design 2.0 of the Multi-Tier Personal Data System

This chapter examines the *Multi-Tier Personal Data System* which represents a case study of program design 2.0, using the structure-behavior coalescence approach. After the software development is finished, the *Multi-Tier Personal Data System* shall appear on a multi-tier platform [Wall04] as shown in Figure 7-1.

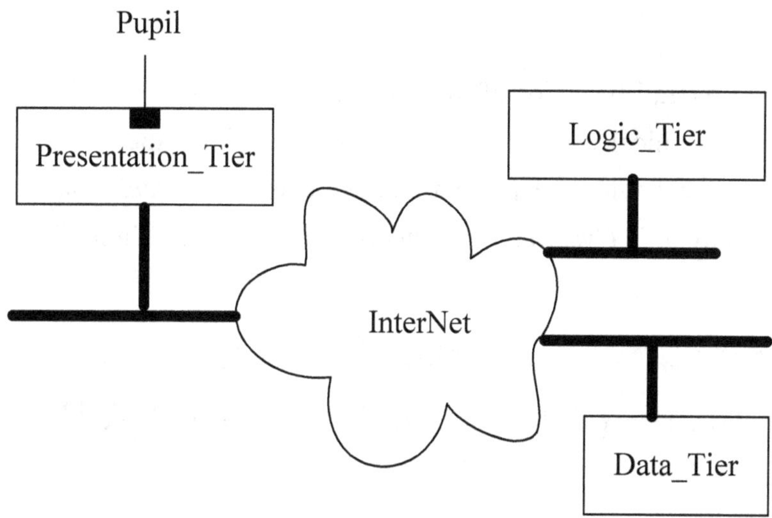

Figure 7-1 *Multi-Tier Personal Data System* on a Multi-Tier Platform

In the *Data_Tier*, there is a *Personal_Database* database [Date03, Elma10] which contains a *Personal_Data* table as shown in Figure 7-2.

Personal Database : Database

Personal_Data : Table

Social_Security_Number	Name	Date_of_Birth	Sex	Height (cm)	Weight (Kg)
318-49-2465	Mary R. Williams	June 17, 1976	Female	165	51
424-87-3651	Lee H. Wulf	July 24, 1982	Female	162	76
512-24-3722	John K. Bryant	May 12, 1954	Male	180	80

Figure 7-2 *Personal_Database* Contains *Personal_Data*

The overall behavior of the *Multi-Tier Personal Data System* is to provide a graphical user interface (GUI) [Gali07] for the *Pupil* actor to trigger two behaviors. The first behavior is *AgeCalculation* and the second behavior is *OverweightCalculation*, as shown in Figure 7-3.

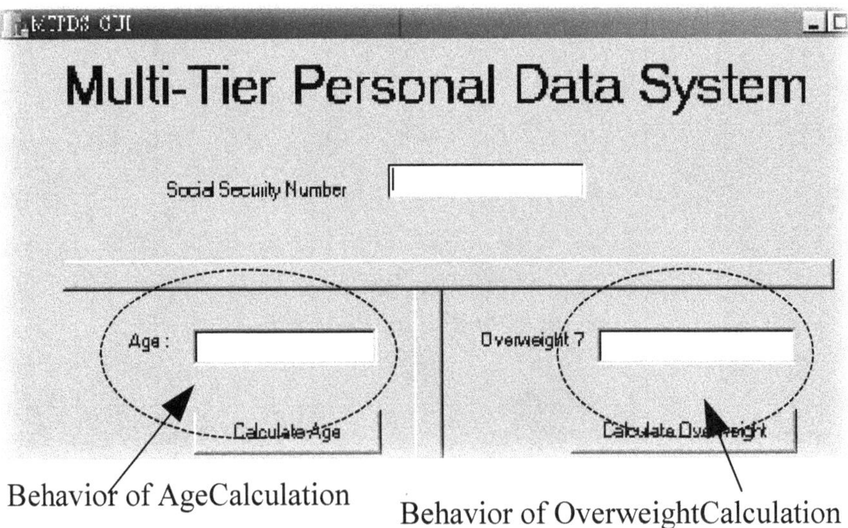

Figure 7-3 Two Behaviors

In the *AgeCalculation* behavior, actor *Pupil* inputs an integer *Social_Security_Number* value then presses down the *Calculate_Age* button. After that, the *Multi-Tier Personal Data System* retrieves the *Date_of_Birth* value from the database in line with the corresponding *Social_Security_Number* value. From the *Date_of_Birth* value, the *Multi-Tier Personal Data System* calculates the *Age* value and displays it on the screen. Figure 7-4 shows the *Social_Security_Number* value is 512-24-3722 and the retrieved *Date_of_Birth* value is May 12, 1954 and the calculated *Age* value, which is 61, is then displayed on the screen.

Personal_Data : Table

Social_Secuirty_Number	Date_of_Birth
318-49-2465	June 17, 1976
424-87-3651	July 24, 1982
512-24-3722	May 12, 1954

the calculated *Age* value when *Date_of_Birth* is May 12, 1954

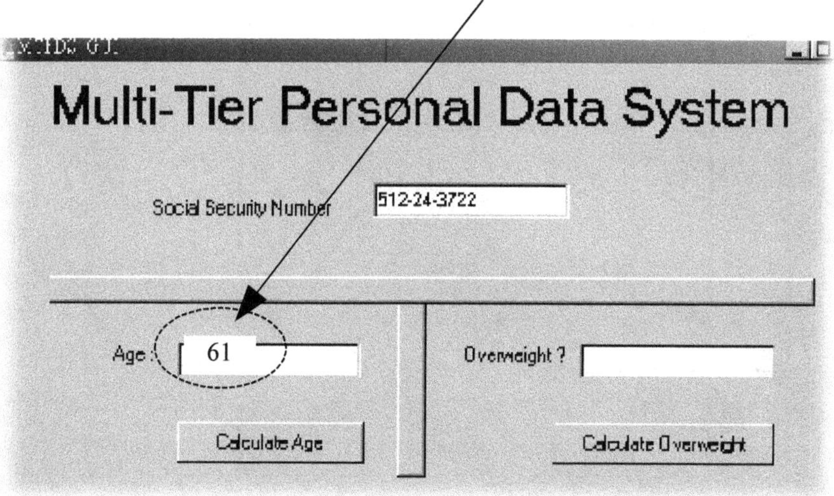

Figure 7-4 Behavior of *AgeCalculation*

In the *OverweightCalculation* behavior, actor *Pupil* inputs an integer *Social_Security_Number* value then presses down the *Calculate_Overweight* button. After that, the *Multi-Tier Personal Data System* retrieves the *Sex*, *Height* and *Weight* values from the database in line with the corresponding *Social_Security_Number* value. From the *Sex*, *Height* and *Weight* values, the *Multi-Tier Personal Data System* calculates the true-or-false Overweight value and displays it on the screen. Figure 7-5 shows the *Social_Security_Number* value is 318-49-2465 and the retrieved *Sex*, *Height* and *Weight* values are Female, 165 and 51, respectively, the calculated Overweight value, which is *No*, is then displayed on the screen.

Personal_Data : Table

Social_Secuirty_Number	Sex	Height (cm)	Weight (Kg)
318-49-2465	Female	165	51
424-87-3651	Female	162	76
512-24-3722	Male	180	80

the calculated *Overweight* value when Sex, Height (cm), and Weight (Kg) are Female, 165, and 51

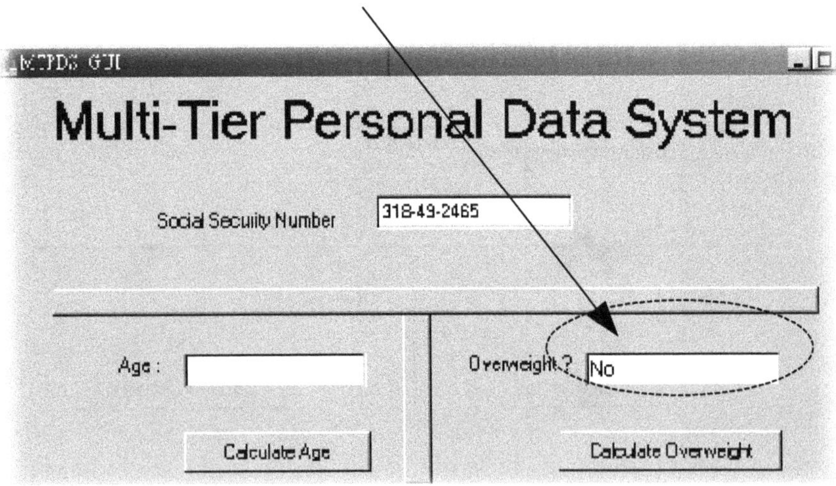

Figure 7-5 Behavior of *OverweightCalculation*

Using the structure-behavior coalescence (SBC) approach, we shall go through: a) framework diagram, b) component operation diagram and c) interaction flow diagram, to accomplish the program design 2.0 of the *Multi-Tier Personal Data System.*

7-1 Framework Diagram

Program design 2.0 uses a framework diagram (FD) to design the multi-layer composition and decomposition of the *Multi-Tier Personal Data System* as shown in Figure 7-6. In the figure, *Presentation_Layer* contains the *MTPDS_GUI* component; *Logic_Layer* contains the *Age_Logic* and *Overweight_Logic* components; *Data_Layer* contains the *Personal_Database* component.

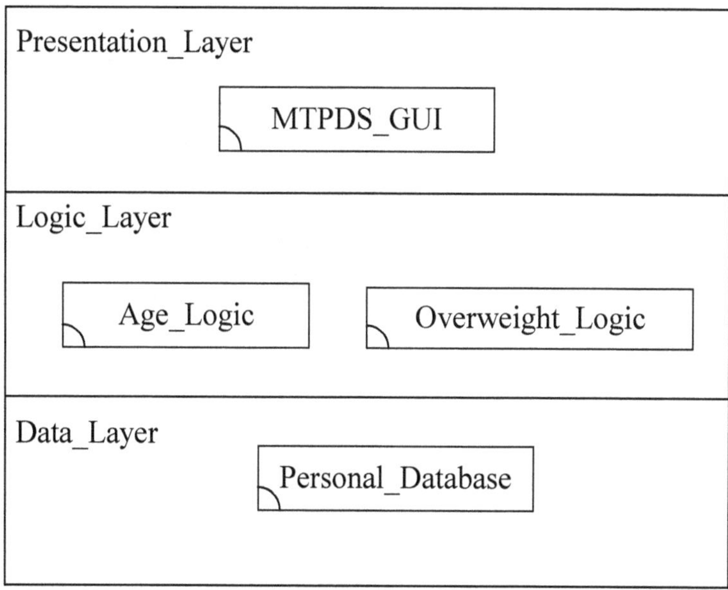

Figure 7-6 FD of the *Multi-Tier Personal Data System*

7-2 Component Operation Diagram

Program design 2.0 uses a component operation diagram (COD) to design the operations of all components of the *Multi-Tier Personal Data System* as shown in Figure 7-7. In the figure, component *MTPDS_GUI* has two operations: *Calculate_AgeClick* and *Calculate_OverweightClick*; component *Age_Logic* has one operation: *Calculate_Age*; component *Overweight_Logic* has one operation: *Calculate_Overweight*; component *Personal_Database* has two operations: *Sql_DateOfBirth_Select* and *Sql_SexHeightWeight_Select*.

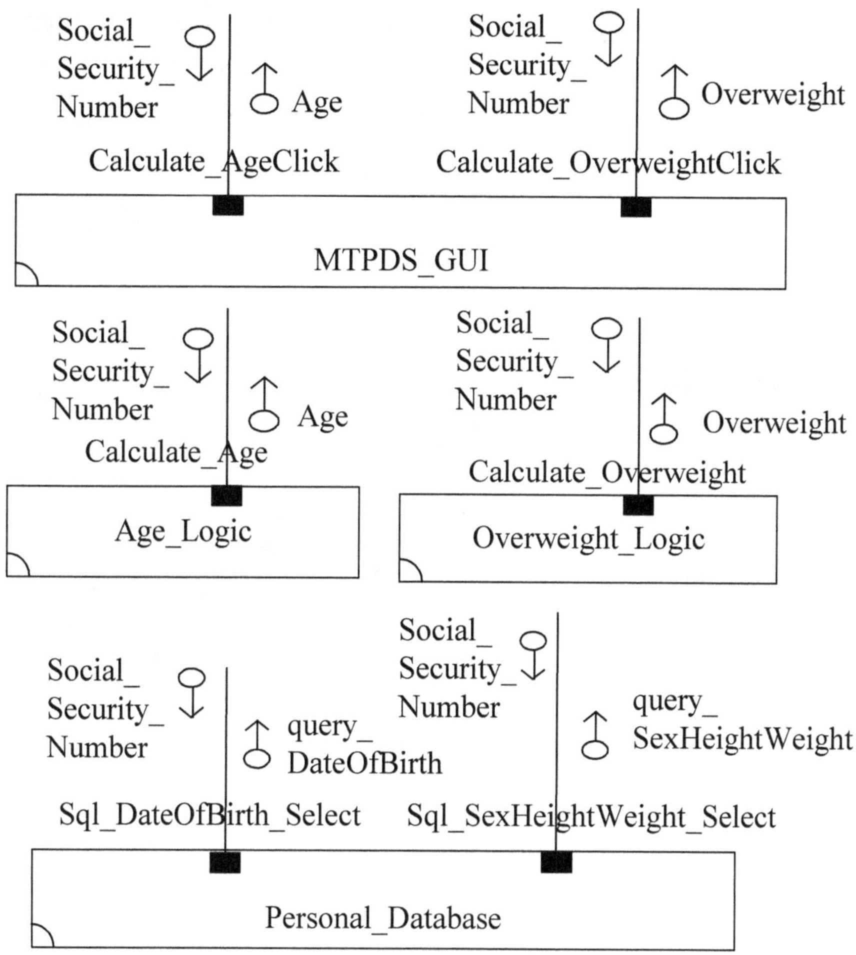

Figure 7-7 COD of the *Multi-Tier Personal Data System*

The operation formula of *Calculate_AgeClick* is *Calculate_AgeClick(In Social_Security_Number; Out Age)*. The operation formula of *Calculate_OverweightClick* is *Calculate_OverweightClick(In Social_Security_Number; Out Overweight)*. The operation formula of *Calculate_Age* is *Calculate_Age(In Social_Security_Number; Out Age)*. The operation formula of *Calculate_Overweight* is *Calculate_Overweight(In Social_Security_Number; Out Overweight)*. The operation formula of *Sql_DateOfBirth_Select* is *Sql_DateOfBirth_Select(In Social_Security_Number; Out query_DateOfBirth)*. The operation formula of *Sql_SexHeightWeight_Select* is *Sql_SexHeightWeight_Select(In Social_Security_Number; Out query_SexHeightWeight)*.

Figure 7-8 shows the primitive data type specification of the *Social_Security_Number* input parameter and the *Age*, *Overweight* output parameters.

Parameter	Data Type	Instances
Social_Security_Number	Text	424-87-3651
Age	Integer	28, 56
Overweight	Boolean	Yes, No

Figure 7-8 Primitive Data Type Specification

Figure 7-9 shows the composite data type specification of the *query_DateOfBirth* output parameter occurring in the *Sql_DateOfBirth_Select(In Social_Security_Number; Out query_DateOfBirth)* operation formula.

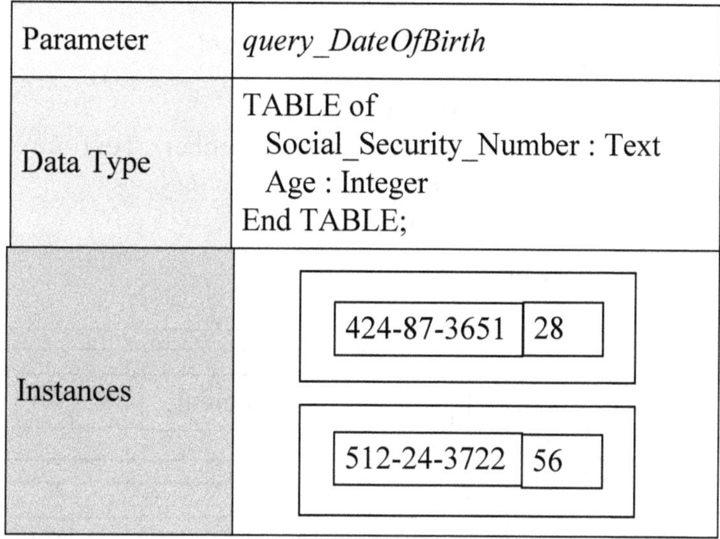

Parameter	*query_DateOfBirth*
Data Type	TABLE of Social_Security_Number : Text Age : Integer End TABLE;
Instances	424-87-3651	28 512-24-3722	56

Figure 7-9 Composite Data Type Specification

Figure 7-10 shows the composite data type specification of the *query_SexHeightWeight* output parameter occurring in the *Sql_SexHeightWeight_Select(In Social_Security_Number; Out query_SexHeightWeight)* operation formula.

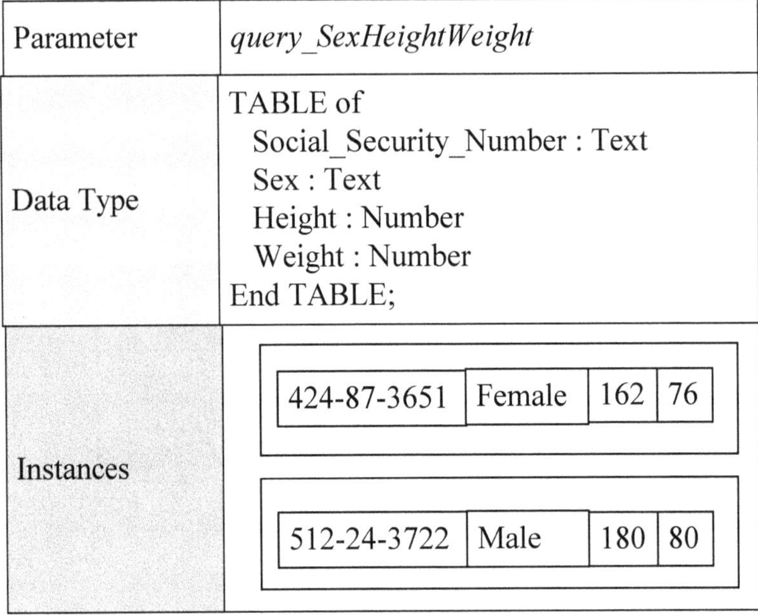

Parameter	*query_SexHeightWeight*
Data Type	TABLE of Social_Security_Number : Text Sex : Text Height : Number Weight : Number End TABLE;
Instances	424-87-3651 | Female | 162 | 76 512-24-3722 | Male | 180 | 80

Figure 7-10 Composite Data Type Specification

7-3 Interaction Flow Diagram

The overall behavior of the *Multi-Tier Personal Data System* includes two individual behaviors: *AgeCalculation* and *OverweightCalculation*. Each individual behavior is represented by an execution path. Program design 2.0 uses an IFD to design each one of these execution paths.

Figure 7-11 shows an IFD of the *AgeCalculation* behavior. First, actor *Pupil* interacts with the *MTPDS_GUI* component through the *Calculate_AgeClick* operation call interaction, carrying the *Social_Security_Number* input parameter. Next, component *MTPDS_GUI* interacts with the *AgeCalculation* component through the

Calculate_Age operation call interaction, carrying the *Social_Security_Number* input parameter. Continuingly, component *Age_Logic* interacts with the *Personal_Database* component through the *Sql_DateOfBirth_Select* operation call interaction, carrying the *Social_Security_Number* input parameter and the *query_DateOfBirth* output parameter. Repeatedly, component *MTPDS_GUI* interacts with the *Age_Logic* component through the *Calculate_Age* operation return interaction, carrying the *Age* output parameter. Finally, actor *Pupil* interacts with the *MTPDS_GUI* component through the *Calculate_AgeClick* operation return interaction, carrying the *Age* output parameter.

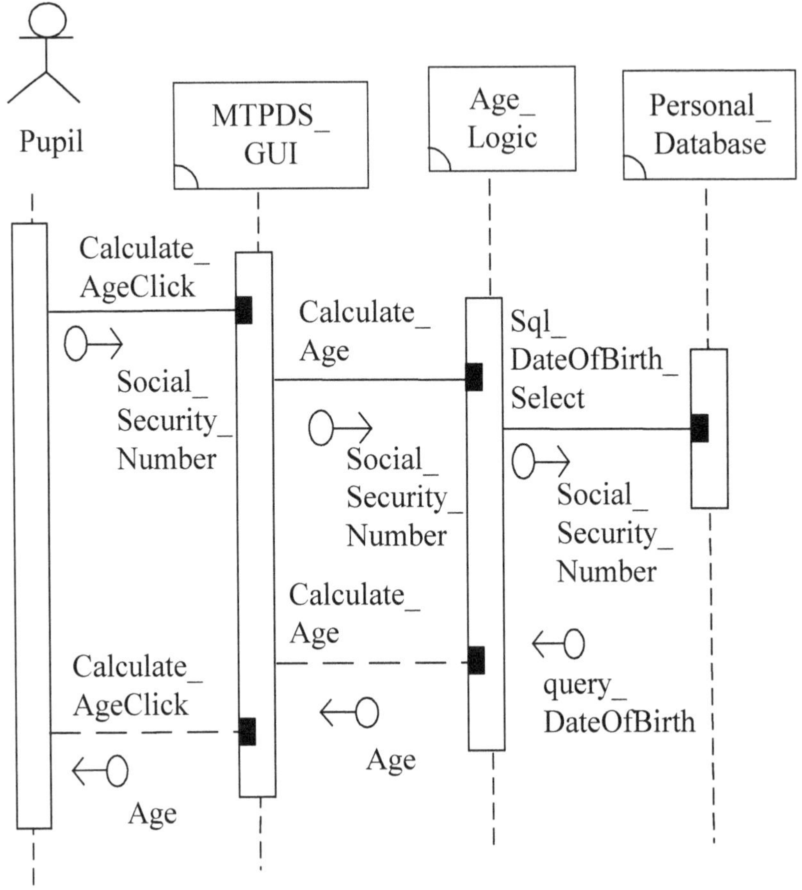

Figure 7-11 IFD of the *AgeCalculation* Behavior

Figure 7-12 shows an IFD of the *OverweightCalculation* behavior. First, actor *Pupil* interacts with the *MTPDS_GUI* component through the *Calculate_OverweightClick* operation call interaction, carrying the *Social_Security_Number* input parameter. Next, component *MTPDS_GUI* interacts with the *OverweightCalculation* component through the *Calculate_Overweight* operation call interaction, carrying the *Social_Security_Number* input parameter. Continuingly, component

Overweight_Logic interacts with the *Personal_Database* component through the *Sql_SexHeightWeight_Select* operation call interaction, carrying the *Social_Security_Number* input parameter and the *query_SexHeightWeight* output parameter. Repeatedly, component *MTPDS_GUI* interacts with the *Overweight_Logic* component through the *Calculate_Overweight* operation return interaction, carrying the *Overweight* output parameter. Finally, actor *Pupil* interacts with the *MTPDS_GUI* component through the *Calculate_OverweightClick* operation return interaction, carrying the *Overweight* output parameter.

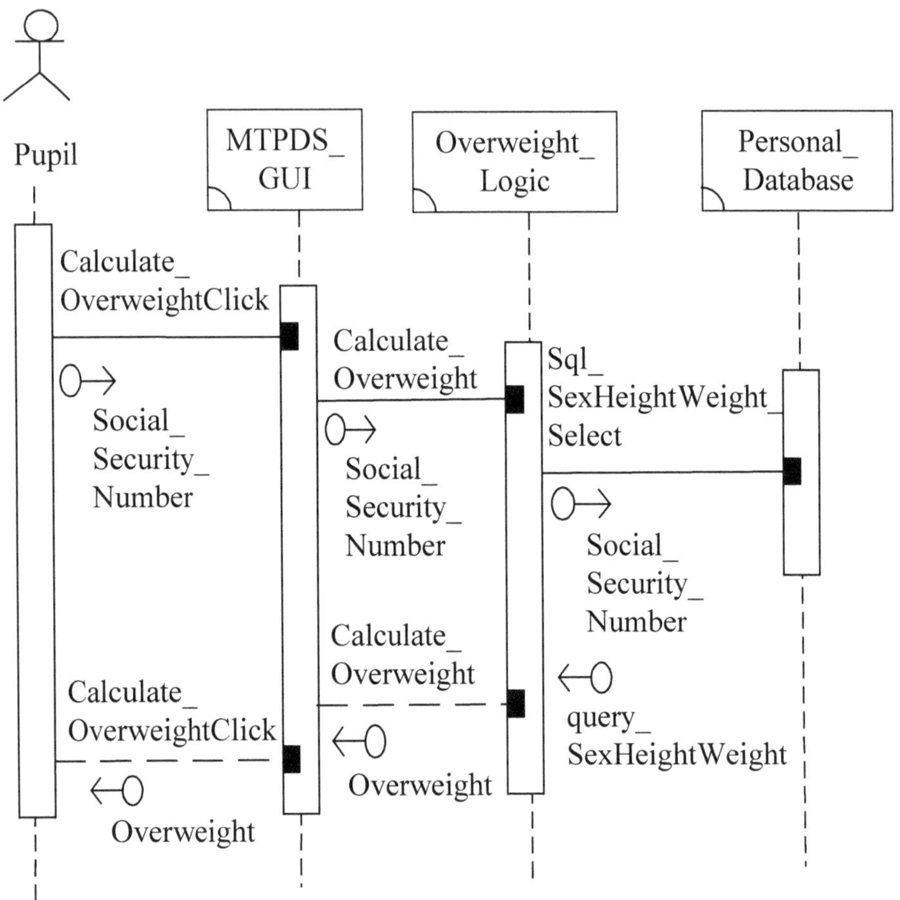

Figure 7-12 IFD of the *OverweightCalculation* Behavior

Chapter 8: Program Design 2.0 of the Unix-like Operating System

This chapter examines the *Unix-like Operating System* which represents a case study of program design 2.0, using the structure-behavior coalescence approach. An operating system is the software that is mounted on top of the computer hardware and used by different user's application programs [Silb08, Tane06], as shown in Figure 8-1.

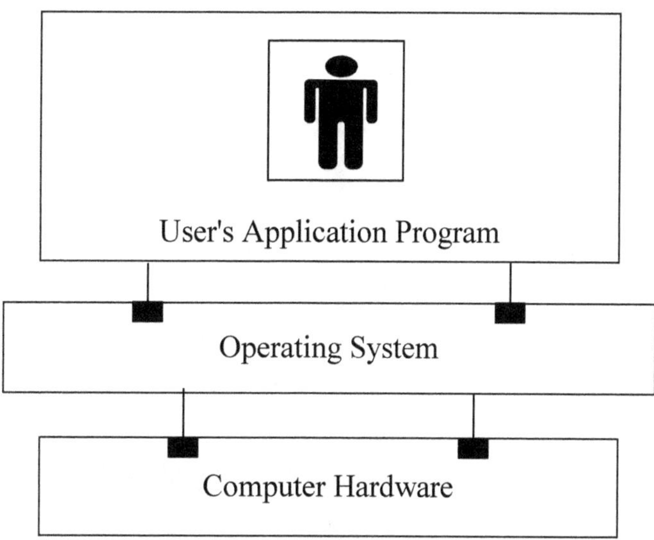

Figure 15-1 Usage of an Operating System

The main purpose of the operating system is an effective way to manage the computer hardware used by the application program. In general, the computer hardware managed by the operating system includes: central process unit (CPU), device, memory and file. For each managed computer hardware there is a corresponding portion of operating system as shown in Figure 8-2.

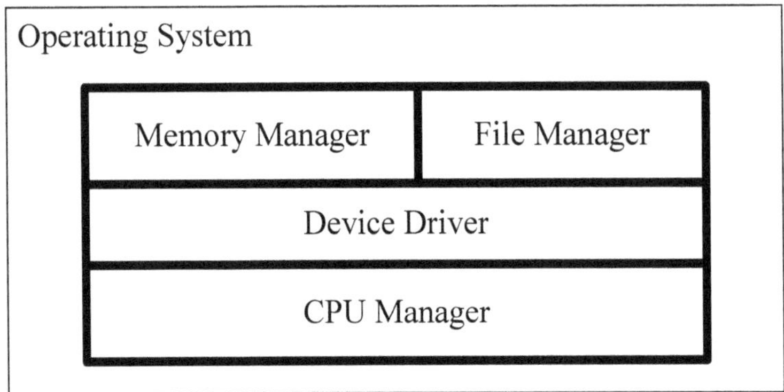

Figure 15-2 Corresponding Portion of Operating System for Each Computer Hardware

There are several CPUs, usually only one in most cases, for many application programs to use. A process stands for a program, such as application program (AP), server program, or device driver program, running on the CPU. The central theme of the CPU manager is a fair usage of CPU resources among these processes. *Unix-Like Operating System* adopts a multi-layer process scheduling algorithm. The scheduler maintains three priority queues of runnable processes, one for each layer, as shown in Figure 8-3. Processes of device driver program are queued in the highest priority layer; processes of server program are in the second; processes of application program are in the lowest. The array *Rdy_Head* has one entry for each queue, with that entry pointing to the process at the head of the queue. Similarly, *Rdy_Tail* is an array whose entries point to the last process on each queue.

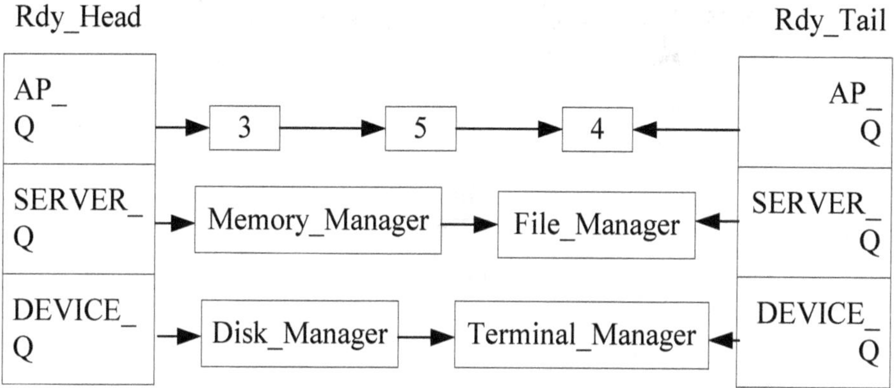

Figure 8-3 Process Scheduling Maintains Three Priority Queues

Whenever a blocked process is awakened, it is put on the end of its queue. The array *Rdy_Tail* makes adding a process at the end of a queue efficient. Whenever a running process becomes blocked, or a runnable process is killed by a signal, that process is removed from the scheduler's queues. Only runnable processes are queued. Given the queue structures just described, the scheduling algorithm is simple: find the highest priority queue that is not empty and pick the process at the head of that queue. If all the queues are empty, the idle routine is run.

Besides process scheduling, CPU manager also provides an operation of interrupt handling to catch interrupts from the I/O devices. Figure 8-4 shows all those operations provided by the CPU manager.

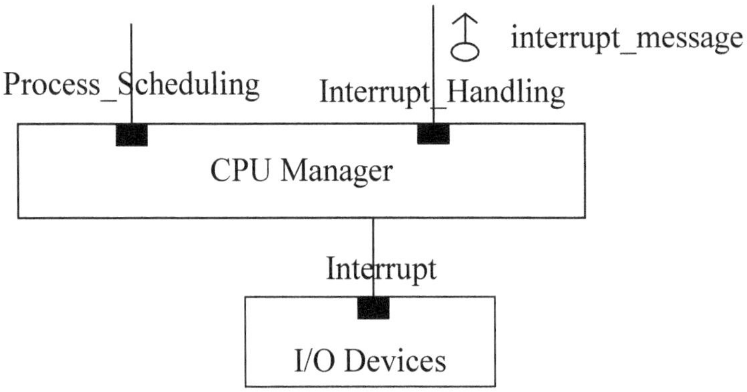

Figure 8-4 Operations Provided by the CPU Manager

Device driver, also playing an important role in the *Unix-Like Operating System*, is to control all the computer's input/output (I/O) peripherals such as disk device and terminal device. Disk manager takes care of the disk devices and terminal manager takes care of the terminal devices. As shown in Figure 8-5, device driver usually issues commands to the I/O devices, takes care interrupt handling message from the CPU manager, and handles errors.

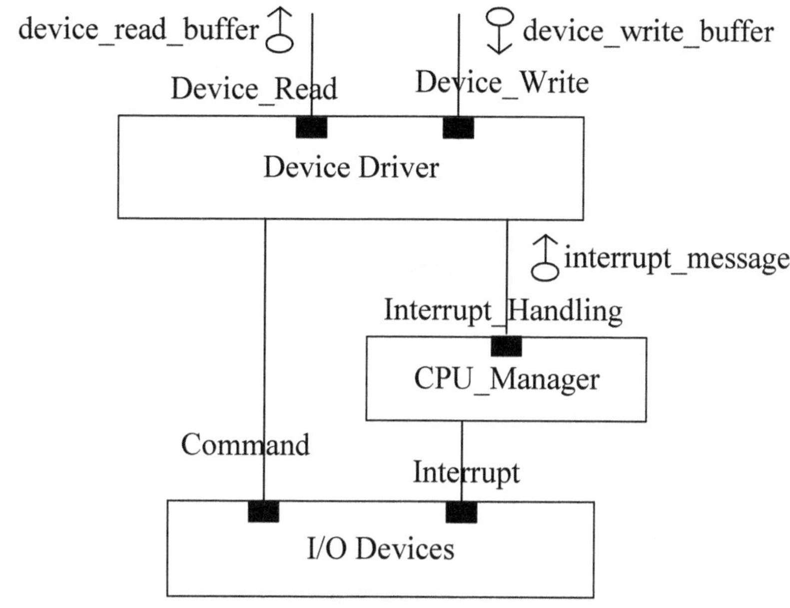

Figure 8-5 Device Driver Interacts with the I/O Devices and CPU Manager

Server programs include: memory manager and file manager. Memory is also an important resource that must be carefully managed. The part of *Unix-Like Operating System* that manages memory is called the memory manager. Memory manager maintains a list of holes sorted in memory address order. Figure 8-6 shows that memory is allocated or deallocated when processes are created or destroyed due to a *Do_Fork* or an *Do_Exit* system call from the application program. When memory is needed the list of holes is searched using first fit for a piece that is big enough to hold the new process. Once a process has been placed in memory, it remains in exactly the same place until it terminates. It is never swapped out and also never moved to another place in memory. Nor does the allocated area ever grow or shrink.

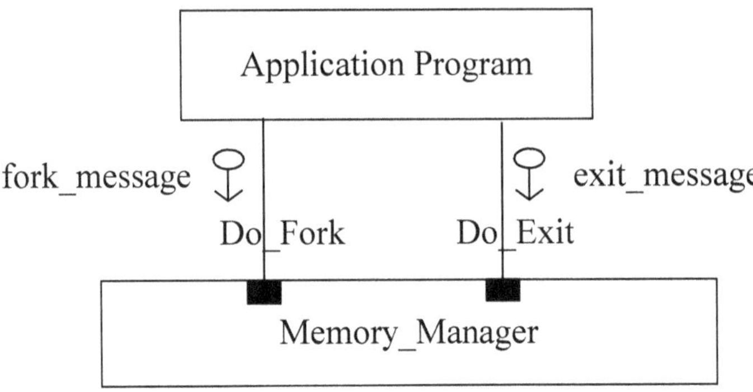

Figure 8-6 Fork/Exit System Calls from the *Application Program*

The most visible part of *Unix-Like Operating System* is the file manager. Most application programs read or write at least one file, and users are always aware of the existence of files and their properties. File manager provides File_Read and File_Write system calls for the application programs to use as shown in Figure 8-7.

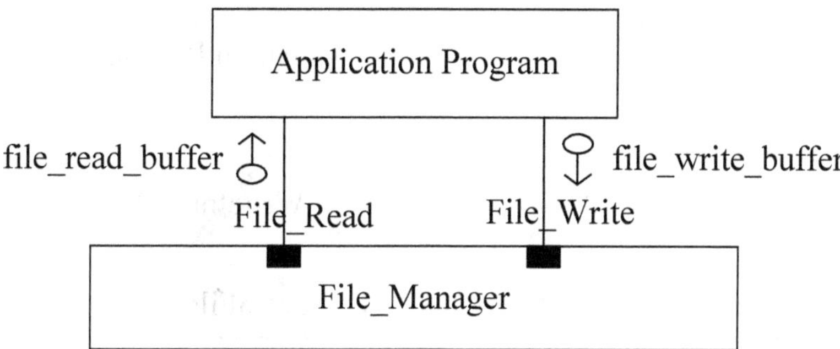

Figure 8-7 File_Read/File_Write System Calls from the *Application Program*

With the CPU manager, device driver, memory manager and file manager, functionality of the *Unix-like Operating System* is represented by the following behaviors: *Login*, *ForkProcess*, *ProcessExit*, *ReadFromFile* and *WriteIntoFile*, as shown in Figure 8-8.

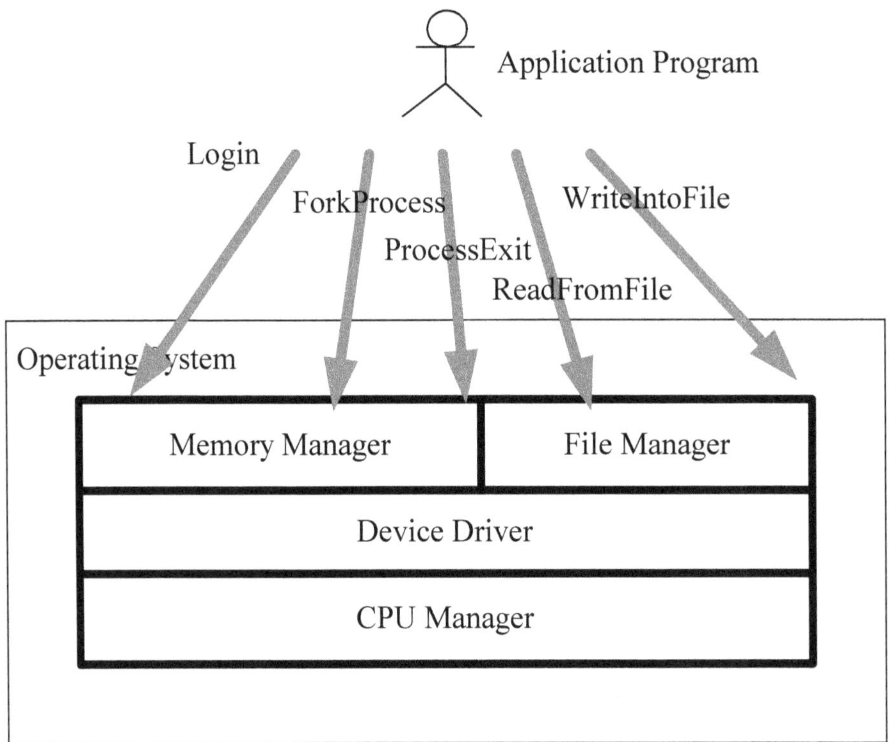

Figure 8-8 Behaviors of the *Unix-Like Operating System*

In the *Login* behavior, *Unix-Like Operating System* waits for a valid user account to be typed at the terminal. In the *ForkProcess* behavior, *Unix-Like Operating System* forks a new child process from the old parent process. In the *ProcessExit* behavior, *Unix-Like Operating System* permits a process to exit. In the *ReadFromFile* behavior, *Unix-Like Operating System* helps an application program read some data from a file. In the *WriteIntoFile* behavior, *Unix-Like Operating System* helps an application program write some data into a file.

Using the structure-behavior coalescence (SBC) approach, we shall go through: a) framework diagram, b) component operation diagram and c) interaction flow diagram, to accomplish the program design 2.0 of the *Unix-Like Operating System*.

8-1 Framework Diagram

Program design 2.0 uses a framework diagram (FD) to design the multi-layer composition and decomposition of the *Unix-Like Operating System* as shown in Figure 8-9. In the figure, *Server_Layer* contains the *Memory_Manager* and *File_Manager* components; *Device_Driver_Layer* contains the *Terminal_Manager* and *Disk_Manager* components; *CPU_Layer* contains the *CPU_Manager* component.

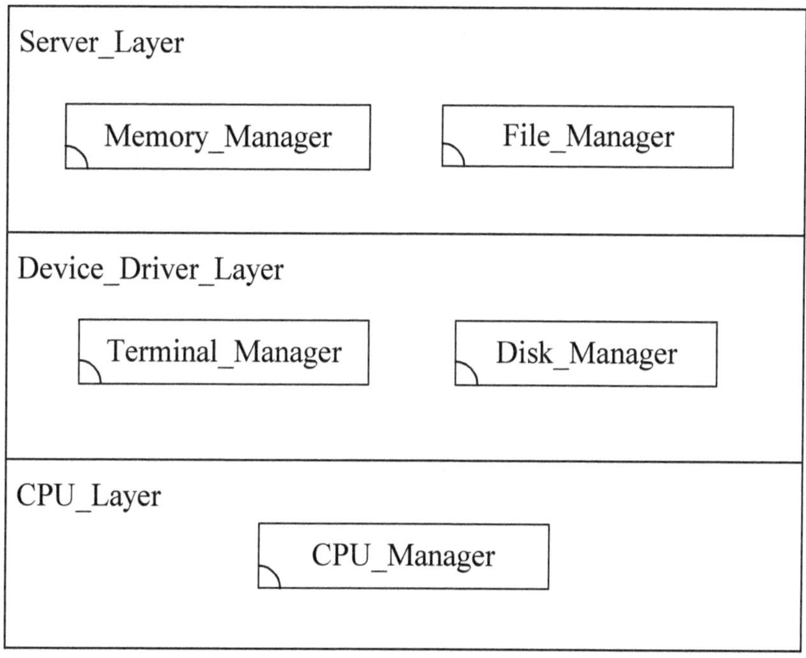

Figure 8-9 FD of the *Unix-Like Operating System*

8-2 Component Operation Diagram

Program design 2.0 uses a component operation diagram (COD) to design the operations of all components of the *Unix-Like Operating System* as shown in Figure 8-10. In the figure, component *Memory_Manager* has two operations: *Do_Fork* and *Do_Exit*; component *File_Manager* has one operation: *File_Read*; component *Terminal_Manager* has two operations: *Terminal_Read* and *Terminal_Write*; component *Disk_Manager* has two operations: *Disk_Read* and *Disk_Write*; component *CPU_Manager* has two operations: *Process_Scheduling* and *Interrupt_Handling*.

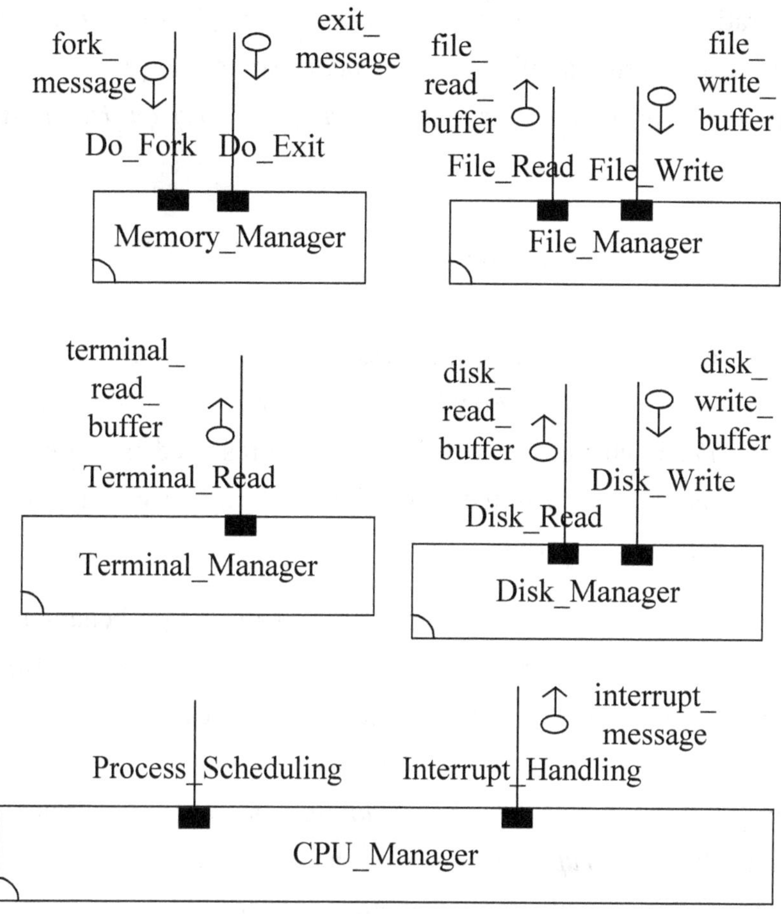

Figure 8-10 COD of the *Unix-Like Operating System*

The operation formula of *Do_Fork* is *Do_Fork(In fork_message)*. The operation formula of *Do_Exit* is *Do_Exit(In exit_message)*. The operation formula of *Do_Exit* is *Do_Exit(In exit_message)*. The operation formula of *File_Read* is *File_Read(Out file_read_buffer)*. The operation formula of *File_Write* is *File_Write(In file_write_buffer)*. The operation formula of *Terminal_Read* is *Terminal_Read(Out terminal_read_buffer)*.

The operation formula of *Disk_Read* is *Disk_Read(Out disk_read_buffer)*. The operation formula of *Disk_Write* is *Disk_Write(In disk_write_buffer)*. The operation formula of *Process_Scheduling* is *Process_Scheduling*. The operation formula of *Interrupt_Handling* is *Interrupt_Handling(Out interrupt_message)*.

8-3 Interaction Flow Diagram

The overall behavior of the *Unix-Like Operating System* includes five behaviors: *Login*, *ForkProcess*, *ProcessExit*, *ReadFromFile*, *WriteIntoFile*. Each individual behavior is represented by an execution path. Program design 2.0 uses an IFD to design each one of these execution paths.

Figure 8-11 shows the design's IFD of the *Login* behavior. First, actor *Application Program* interacts with the *Terminal_Manager* component through the *Terminal_Read* operation call interaction. Next, component *Terminal_Manager* interacts with the *CPU_Manager* component through the *Interrupt_Handling* operation call interaction, carrying the *interrupt_message* output parameter. Finally, actor *Application Program* interacts with the *Terminal_Manager* component through the *Terminal_Read* operation return interaction, carrying the *terminal_read_buffer* output parameter.

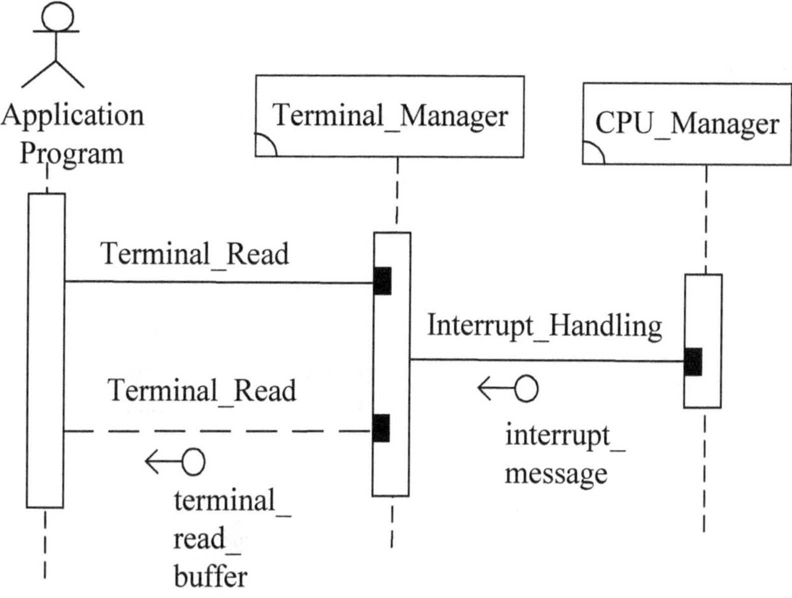

Figure 8-11 IFD of the *Login* Behavior

Figure 8-12 shows the design's IFD of the *ForkProcess* behavior. Actor *Application Program* interacts with the *Memory_Manager* component through the *Do_Fork* operation call interaction, carrying the *fork_message* input parameter.

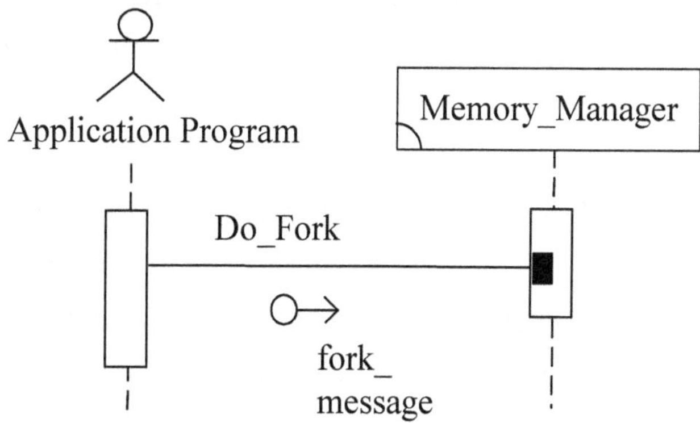

Figure 8-12 IFD of the *ForkProcess* Behavior

Figure 8-13 shows the design's IFD of the *ProcessExit* behavior. Actor *Application Program* interacts with the *Memory_Manager* component through the *Do_Exit* operation call interaction, carrying the *exit_message* input parameter.

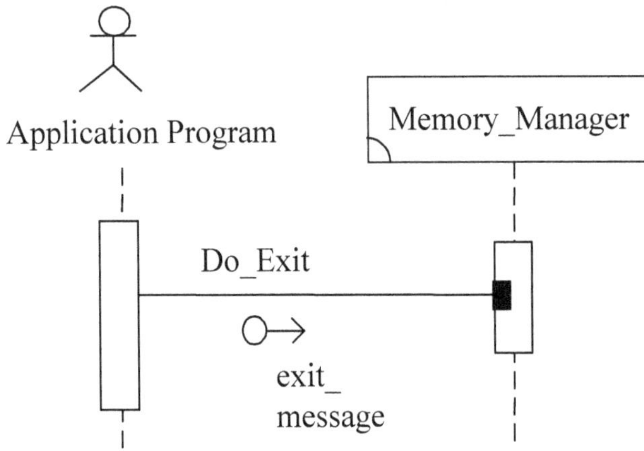

Figure 8-13 IFD of the *ProcessExit* Behavior

Figure 8-14 shows the design's IFD of the *ReadFromFile* behavior. First, actor *Application Program* interacts with the *File_Manager* component through the *File_Read* operation call interaction. Next, component *File_Manager* interacts with the *Disk_Manager* component through the *Disk_Read* operation call interaction. Continuingly, component *Disk_Manager* interacts with the *CPU_Manager* component through the *Interrupt_Handling* operation call interaction, carrying the *interrupt_message* output parameter. Repeatedly, component *File_Manager* interacts with the *Disk_Manager* component through the *Disk_Read* operation return interaction, carrying the *disk_read_buffer* output parameter. Finally, actor *Application Program* interacts with the *File_Manager* component through the *File_Read* operation return interaction, carrying the *file_read_buffer* output parameter.

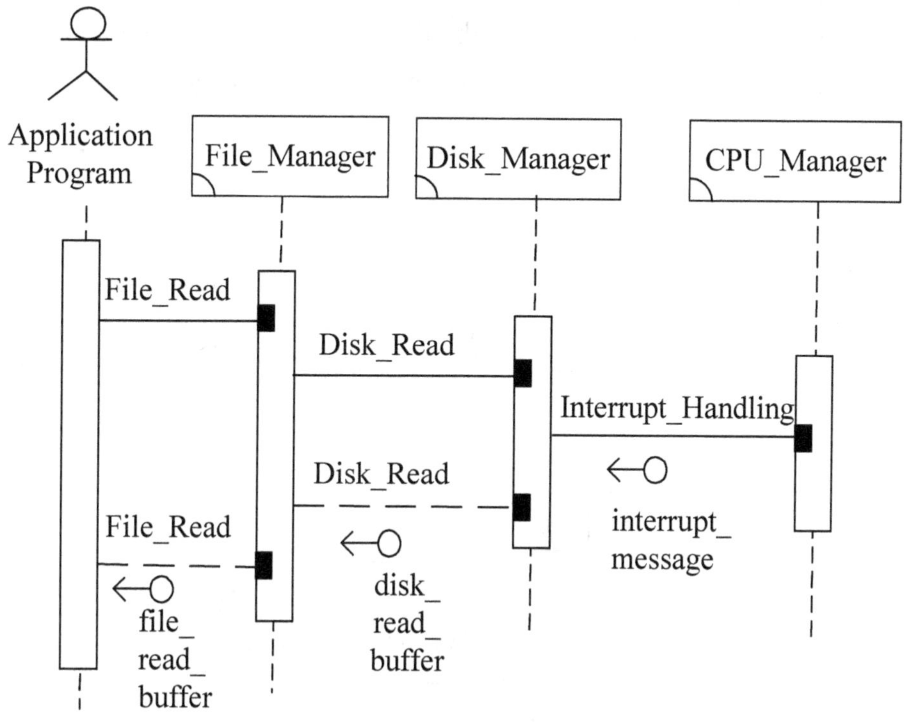

Figure 8-14 IFD of the *ReadFromFile* Behavior

Figure 8-15 shows the design's IFD of the *WriteIntoFile* behavior. First, actor *Application Program* interacts with the *File_Manager* component through the *File_Write* operation call interaction. Next, component *File_Manager* interacts with the *Disk_Manager* component through the *Disk_Write* operation call interaction. Continuingly, component *Disk_Manager* interacts with the *CPU_Manager* component through the *Interrupt_Handling* operation call interaction, carrying the *interrupt_message* output parameter. Repeatedly, component *File_Manager* interacts with the *Disk_Manager* component through the *Disk_Write* operation return interaction, carrying the *disk_write_buffer* output parameter. Finally, actor *Application Program* interacts with the *File_Manager* component through the *File_Write* operation return interaction, carrying the *file_write_buffer* output parameter.

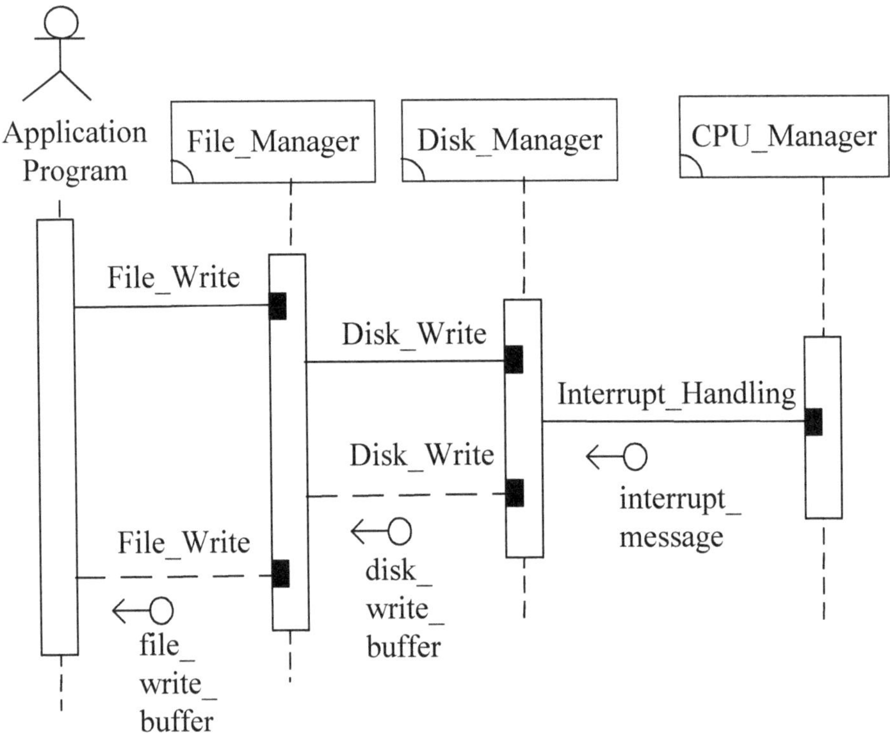

Figure 8-15 IFD of the *WriteIntoFile* Behavior

APPENDIX A: PROGRAM DESIGN 2.0

(1) Framework Diagram

Presentation Layer

Logic Layer

Data Layer

: Component

(2) Component Operation Diagram

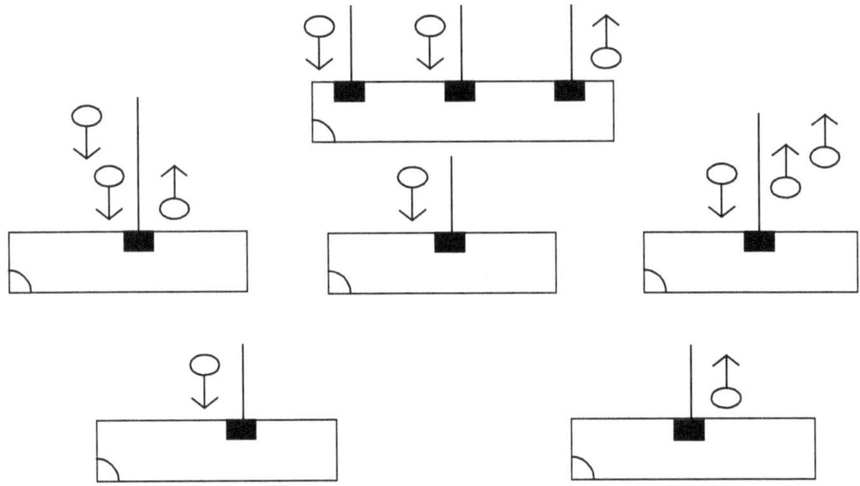

: Operation

: Input Data

: Output Data

: Component

(3) Interaction Flow Diagram

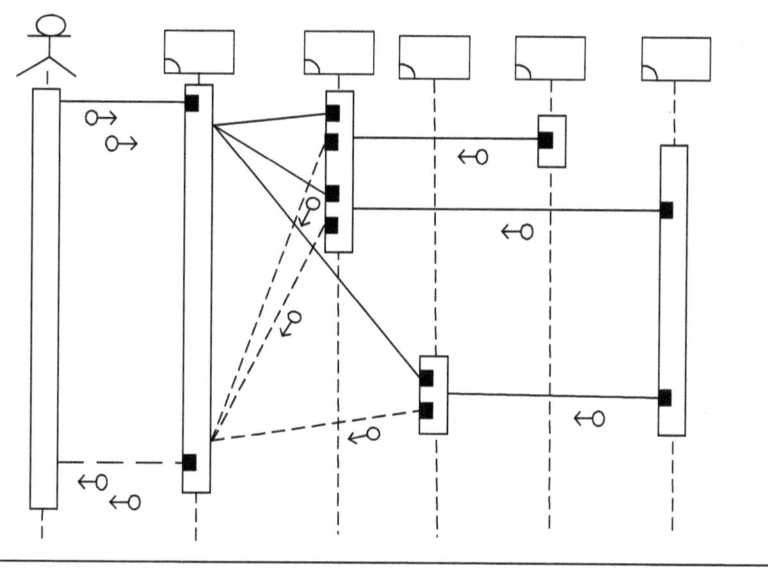

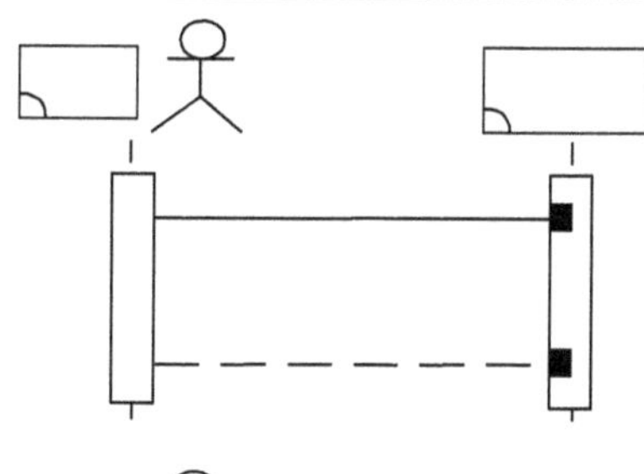

: Operation Call Interaction

: Operation Return Interaction

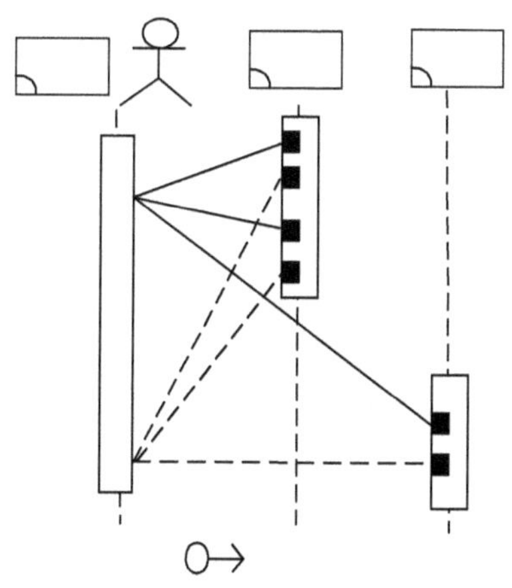

: Conditional
Operation Call Interaction

: Conditional
Operation Return Interaction

O→ : Input Data

←O : Output Data

APPENDIX B: SBC PROCESS ALGEBRA

(1) Operation-Based Single-Queue SBC Process Algebra

(1) <System> ::= "**fix**(" <Process_Variable> "="<IFD> "•" <Process_Variable>
{"+" <IFD> "•" <Process_Variable>} ")"

(2) <IFD> ::= <Type_1_Interaction> {"•" <Type_1_Or_2_Interaction>}

(3) <Type_1_Or_2_Interaction> ::= <Type_1_Interaction>
| <Type_2_Interaction>

(2) Operation-Based Multi-Queue SBC Process Algebra

(1) <System> ::= <FixIFD> {"|| " <FixIFD>}

(2) <FixIFD> ::= "**fix**(" <Process_Variable>"="<IFD>
"•" <Process_Variable> ")"

(3) <IFD> ::= <Type_1_Interaction> {"• " Type_1_Or_2_Interaction>}

(4) <Type_1_Or_2_Interaction> ::= <Type_1_Interaction>

| <Type_2_Interaction>

(3) Operation-Based Infinite-Queue SBC Process Algebra

(1) <System> ::= "! ("<IFD> " • " *STOP* ")" {"|| ! (" <IFD> " • " *STOP* ")"}

(2) <IFD> ::= <Type_1_Interaction> {"• " <Type_1_Or_2_Interaction>}

(3) <Type_1_Or_2_Interaction> ::= <Type_1_Interaction>

| <Type_2_Interaction>

BIBLIOGRAPHY

[Ashw90] Ashworth, C., *SSADM : A Practical Approach*, 1st Edition, McGraw-Hill Book Company (UK) Ltd., 1990.

[Booc07] Booch, G.. et al,. *Object-Oriented Analysis and Design with Applications*, 3rd Edition, Addison-Wesley Professional, 2007.

[Came89] Cameron, John R., *The Jackson Approach to Software Development*, IEEE Computer Society Press, 1989.

[Chao14a] Chao, W. S., *Systems Thingking 2.0: Architectural Thinking Using the SBC Architecture Description Language*, CreateSpace Independent Publishing Platform, 2014.

[Chao14b] Chao, W. S., *General Systems Theory 2.0: General Architectural Theory Using the SBC Architecture*, CreateSpace Independent Publishing Platform, 2014.

[Chao14c] Chao, W. S., *Software Modeling and Architecting: Structure-Behavior Coalescence for Software Architecture*, CreateSpace Independent Publishing Platform, 2014.

[Chao15a] Chao, W. S., *Theoretical Foundations of Structure-Behavior Coalescence*, CreateSpace Independent Publishing Platform, 2015.

[Chao15b] Chao, W. S., *Variants of Interaction Flow Diagrams*, CreateSpace Independent Publishing Platform, 2015.

[Chao15c] Chao, W. S., *A Process Algebra For Systems Architecture: The Structure-Behavior Coalescence Approach*, CreateSpace Independent Publishing Platform, 2015.

[Chao15d] Chao, W. S., *An Observation Congruence Model For Systems Architecture: The Structure-Behavior Coalescence Approach*, CreateSpace Independent Publishing Platform, 2015.

[Chao15e] Chao, W. S., *Variants of SBC Process Algebra: The Structure-Behavior Coalescence Approach*, CreateSpace Independent Publishing Platform, 2015.

[Chao17a] Chao, W. S., *Channel-Based Single-Queue SBC Process Algebra For Systems Definition: General Architectural Theory at Work*, CreateSpace Independent Publishing Platform, 2017.

[Chao17b] Chao, W. S., *Channel-Based Multi-Queue SBC Process Algebra For Systems Definition: General Architectural Theory at Work*, CreateSpace Independent Publishing Platform, 2017.

[Chao17c] Chao, W. S., *Channel-Based Infinite-Queue SBC Process Algebra For Systems Definition: General Architectural Theory at Work*, CreateSpace Independent Publishing Platform, 2017.

[Chao17d] Chao, W. S., *Operation-Based Single-Queue SBC Process Algebra For Systems Definition: General Architectural Theory at Work*, CreateSpace Independent Publishing Platform, 2017.

[Chao17e] Chao, W. S., *Operation-Based Multi-Queue SBC Process Algebra For Systems Definition: Unification of Systems Structure and Systems Behavior*, CreateSpace Independent Publishing Platform, 2017.

[Chao17f] Chao, W. S., *Operation-Based Infinite-Queue SBC Process Algebra For Systems Definition: Unification of Systems Structure and Systems Behavior*, CreateSpace Independent Publishing Platform, 2017.

[Chen76] Chen, P. et al., "The Entity-Relationship Model - Toward a Unified View of Data", *ACM Transactions on Database Systems* 1 (1), pp. 9–36, 1976.

[Date03] Date, C. J., *An Introduction to Database Systems*, 8th Edition, Addison Wesley, 2003.

[DeMa79] DeMarco, T., *Structured Analysis and System Specification*, Prentice Hall, 1979.

[Denn 08] Dennis, A. et al., *Systems Analysis and Design*, 4th Edition, Wiley, 2008.

[Dori95] Dori, D., "Object-Process Analysis: Maintaining the Balance between System Structure and Behavior," *Journal of Logic and Computation* 5(2), pp.227-249, 1995.

[Dori02] Dori, D., *Object-Process Methodology: A Holistic Systems Paradigm*, Springer Verlag, New York, 2002.

[Dori16] Dori, D., *Model-Based Systems Engineering with OPM and SysML*, Springer Verlag, New York, 2016.

[Elma10] Elmasri, R., *Fundamentals of Database Systems*, 6th Edition, Addison Wesley, 2010.

[Gali07] Galitz, W., *The Essential Guide to User Interface Design: An Introduction to GUI Design Principles and Techniques*, 3rd

Edition Wiley, 2007.

[Ghar11] Gharajedaghi, J., *Systems Thinking: Managing Chaos and Complexity: A Platform for Designing Business Architecture*, Morgan Kaufmann, 2011.

[Grad13] Grady, J. O., *System Requirements Analysis*, 2nd Edition, Elsevier, 2013.

[Hatl00] Hatley, D. J. 2t al., *Process for System Architecture and Requirements Engineering*, 1st Edition, 2000.

[Hoff10] Hoffer, J. A., et al., *Modern Systems Analysis and Design*, Prentice Hall, 6th Edition, 2010.

[Hoar85] Hoare, C. A. R., *Communicating Sequential Processes*, Prentice-Hall, 1985.

[Jack75] Jackson, M. A., *Principles of Program Design*, 1st Edition, Academic Press, 1975.

[Kend10] Kendall, K. et al., *Systems Analysis and Design*, 8th Edition, Prentice Hall, 2010.

[Marc88] Marca, D. A. et al., *SADT: Structured Analysis and Design Technique,* McGraw-Hill, 1988.

[Miln89] Milner, R., *Communication and Concurrency*, Prentice-Hall, 1989.

[Miln99] Milner, R., *Communicating and Mobile Systems: the π-Calculus*, 1st Edition, Cambridge University Press, 1999.

[Pele00] Peleg, M. et al., "The Model Multiplicity Problem: Experimenting with Real-Time Specification Methods". *IEEE Tran. on Software Engineering*. 26 (8), pp. 742–759, 2000.

[Prat00] Pratt, T. W. et al., *Programming Languages: Design and Implementation*, 4th Edition, Prentice Hall 2000.

[Pres09] Pressman, R. S., *Software Engineering: A Practitioner's Approach*, 7th Edition, McGraw-Hill, 2009.

[Scho10] Scholl, C., *Functional Decomposition with Applications to FPGA Synthesis*, Springer, 2010.

[Seth96] Sethi, R., *Programming Languages: Concepts and Constructs*, 2nd Edition, Addison-Wesley, 1996.

[Shel11] Shelly, G. B., et al., *Systems Analysis and Design*, 9th Edition, Course Technology, 2011.

[Silb08] Silberschatz, A. et al., *Operating System Concepts*, 8th Edition, Wiley, 2008.

[Sode03] Soderborg, N.R. et al., "OPM-based Definitions and Operational Templates," *Communications of the ACM* 46(10), pp. 67-72, 2003.

[Somm06] Sommerville, I., *Software Engineering*, 8th Edition, Addison-Wesley, 2006.

[Tane06] Tanenbaum, A. S. et al., *Operating Systems Design and Implementation*, 3rd Edition, Prentice Hall, 2006.

[Wall04] Wall, D., *Multi-Tier Application Programming with PHP: Practical Guide for Architects and Programmers*, Morgan Kaufmann, 2004.

[Your99] Yourdon, E., *Death March: The Complete Software Developer's Guide to Surviving Mission Impossible Projects*, Prentice-Hall, 1999.

INDEX

N

O

P

S

V

www.ingramcontent.com/pod-product-compliance
Lightning Source LLC
Chambersburg PA
CBHW060157060326
40690CB00018B/4153

* 9 7 8 1 5 2 2 8 4 5 4 5 4 *